30-MINUTE GROUPS

EXECUTIVE FUNCTION

BOOSTING BRAINPOWER, INCREASING PRODUCTIVITY, AND ACHIEVING ACADEMIC SUCCESS

LAURA FILTNESS

NATIONAL CENTER for YOUTH ISSUES

NATIONAL CENTER for YOUTH ISSUES
P.O. Box 22185
Chattanooga, TN 37422-2185
423.899.5714 • 866.318.6294
fax: 423.899.4547 • www.ncyi.org

ISBN: 9781965066126

Written by: Laura Filtness, M.Ed.
Published by National Center for Youth Issues
Printed in the U.S.A. • April 2026

Contents

Introduction

Executive function helps regulate, control, and manage thoughts and actions. It affects key skills like:

- Planning
- Time Management
- Organization
- Task Initiation
- Attention
- Self-Monitoring
- Self-Regulation
- Impulse Control
- Flexible Thinking

Why Is This Important?

Imagine a teacher giving students ten minutes to complete an assignment. One student spends most of that time gathering supplies or getting distracted. When time is up, they haven't finished and feel frustrated. Later, students who completed their work participated in a fun activity, while the students with unfinished work had to complete that work instead, leading to more frustration.

What executive functioning skills could have helped? **All of them!**

- **Time Management** – Understanding how to divide time effectively.
- **Task Initiation** – Starting promptly instead of procrastinating.
- **Organization** – Having materials ready to begin.
- **Planning** – Thinking ahead to complete tasks on time.
- **Self-Monitoring** – Recognizing when we're off-task.
- **Self-Regulation & Flexible Thinking** – Adapting to consequences and shifting mindset.
- **Impulse Control** – Avoiding distractions and staying focused.

About this Curriculum

Designed for **2nd–9th graders**, this program includes 10–12 interactive lessons (30 minutes each) to help students understand and practice executive functioning skills. Lessons are flexible and tailored to different learning styles, ensuring that every student can engage, grow, and apply these essential skills in their daily lives.

The strategic design enables students to empathize, connect with others, and translate their new knowledge into practice. The American School Counselor Association (ASCA®)-aligned curriculum contains an introductory lesson, ten core lessons, and a final closing lesson. Facilitators may include the initial and final lessons as part of the core sessions if they have extra time.

You'll find a range of essential resources in the book's concluding pages. These consist of permission and completion letters, attendance logs, a group expectation form, and a Certificate of Completion. You'll also find pre- and post-group assessments to measure the success of the programming and templates to share the results with interested parties. Moreover, this workbook provides a comprehensive action plan that will integrate effortlessly into your ASCA® evaluation document and facilitate a seamless transition from planning to assessment.

Practical and easy to implement, the activities are designed for both small- and large-group instruction. Most lessons require only basic supplies like pencils, markers or crayons, and scratch paper. A few activities suggest simple, easy-to-find materials to enhance the experience, but no extensive prep is needed. You won't need to spend hours getting ready—everything you need is clearly outlined and easy to gather!

See page 115 for information on Downloadable Resources.

What's Included?

30-Minute Focus: Executive Function offers a comprehensive ten-lesson program and accompanying materials for facilitating group sessions. Following each detailed lesson outline, you'll find practical resources for establishing a small group within your school environment.

Mind Map: Provides an illustrated diagram of the different executive functioning skills or parts of the brain. Students should begin each lesson by brainstorming the skill, considering its meaning or the role of a specific part of the brain. It is optional to write these, but visuals are helpful for many students. Some find it helpful to draw the Mind Map on the board, or you can draw a tree with the concept written on the trunk and the related words on the fruit of the tree.

ASCA® Standards: Each lesson includes success criteria for the learning target.

Lesson Introduction: At the start of each lesson, we will introduce a concept and explain it to provide clarity for the upcoming story.

Circle Time Questions: This section has optional questions for the facilitator to start the conversation. These questions allow students to deepen their understanding of the topic and build community by discussing and sharing their experiences.

Story Time: Provides stories related to the concept that should be read aloud to help children understand the concept.

Coloring Sheets: Allow younger students to visualize the concept. Students can color the sheet while the facilitator shares the initial story, after the lesson is complete, or take it home with them.

Discussion Questions: Students can discuss the questions posed to help them process their beliefs on the subject.

Skill Practice: These interactive and hands-on activities provide students an opportunity to practice the Executive Functioning skills.

Additional Activities: Provides activities to help students practice and apply the lesson concept.

Closing Considerations: This is an opportunity to review the concept and ask students to reflect on their new experience with the material.

Would You Rather? Game: Provides an opportunity for students to consider what they would "rather" do related to the lesson's topic. The facilitator can cut out the cards and let students discuss or read aloud while moving from one side of the room to the other to communicate their preferred answer.

Accompanying Group Documents

Action Plan: Provides the necessary information required to complete the ASCA® National Model's Classroom and Group Mindsets & Behaviors Action Plan.

Permission Form: The permission form is used to gain the permission of the student's caregivers for the child to attend the Executive Functioning Group. Be sure to send this home about two weeks before the group starts.

Group Expectations: These provide basic expectations for the group process. The form has space for the facilitator and group to collaborate on adding additional expectations to fit their group.

Group Attendance Form: This is a blank form that allows the facilitator to track which students attended each session and what topics were discussed.

Group Attendance Form (Example): This form is an example of how to best utilize the group attendance form.

Mindsets & Behaviors Pre- and Post-Assessment: Provides an opportunity for students to share what they know of the concepts before and after they've completed the curriculum.

To measure the progress of students who participate, use the same assessment for both the pre-group and post-group assessment. Administer the pre-group assessment at the start of the instructional period, followed by instruction and practice opportunities for measured skills or knowledge.

At the end of the instructional period, administer the post-group assessment and compare the results of both assessments to identify areas of improvement and areas that need further instruction. Then calculate the average score of the pre-assessment and post-assessment and determine the percentage of improvement by subtracting the pre-assessment average from the post-assessment average and then dividing the result by the pre-assessment total. Use this pre-assessment average improvement to measure the students' progress effectively.

Percentage of Improvement Formula

((Post-Assessment Total - Pre-Assessment Total) / Pre-Assessment Total)) x 100 = Percentage of Overall Improvement

Example:

((30 Post-Assessment Total - 18 Pre-Assessment Total) / 18)) x 100 = 66.67% Overall Improvement

Look at your data to determine who should attend your group. Review referrals, attendance data, and achievement metrics and look for students with challenges. Consider also tracking students' academic achievements, absences, and discipline referrals. You can better see the impact of your small groups when strategically selecting students and closely monitoring their academic, attendance, and conduct metrics. Be sure to share the results of your intervention with your advisory council.

Results Report: The Results Report shows one way to share your data with interested parties. Remember, we want to be sure to use graphs and charts because they show our data, which has more impact than a paragraph of text. Use whatever platform you prefer to show your data, but be sure to complete the data following the group, and then share it with interested parties.

Results Report (Example): The Results Report (Example) shows what your data might resemble following the completion of the groups. You can use this form to share your data.

Certificate of Completion: Present students with a certificate to congratulate them on completing the curriculum.

Executive Function Group Completion Letter: This Letter is written to the caregivers/guardians of students following the completion of the group. Provide students with their certificates and their group review letters during the last session.

Additional Materials: We promised to provide everything you need in this workbook, and we have. However, you will need to make copies of the pre- and post-group assessments, the activity sheets you choose to use, and print the coloring sheets, if appropriate for your group. You might also print and cut out the "Would You Rather?" game or facilitate that activity verbally. We recommend having crayons and pencils readily available on the table. It might also be helpful to have some fidgets accessible for your students during their group session.

Other optional materials include:

- Chapter three lesson on planning/prioritizing: Highlighters or crayons in yellow, green, and pink and a stopwatch (or use your phone)
- Chapter four lesson on organization: colored sticker dots, Washi tape, and have students bring their own backpacks
- Chapter five lesson on focus: windchime, cups (2 per student), and colored pom poms in a variety of colors
- Chapter seven lesson on mindset: bubbles and a mini shredder
- Chapter eight lesson on self-regulation: music of your choice
- Final session: note cards and pom-poms

Good luck with your group! We hope you have a fantastic experience!

Introductory Group Session

Directions & Overview

Conduct this introductory session before starting the regular lessons. This initial meeting will acclimate students to the program's structure, expectations, and foundational tools. They will learn the brain model and check-in process that they will utilize in each subsequent session.

Directions: Begin by extending a warm welcome to all participants. Communicate the group's objectives and generate enthusiasm for learning and collaboration.

Introductions: Foster a sense of community by encouraging students to share their names and something about themselves, or by playing a quick game of "Two Truths and a Lie."

Begin the group by asking members to share a **Peak** and **Pit** from their week.

Share a positive or high moment from the week. Something that made you smile or feel good.

Share a low from the week. How did you get through it?

Alternatively, students can use an emotion scale to rate their feelings on a scale of 1 (not feeling great) to 10 (feeling their best).

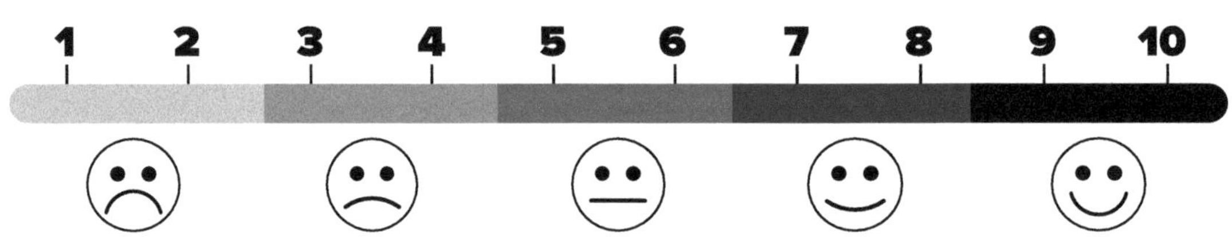

Explain the Group Format: Explain how often the group will meet, when you will meet, and the list of topics students will be learning about. Each week, it's important to review the schedule of activities you have planned with students (e.g., reading, sharing, playing a game). If run as a lunch bunch, clarify with students that they will eat while engaging in an activity like listening to a story or working on a coloring sheet. Each session should end with a student reflection—a one-sentence summary of what they learned and how they plan to apply it.

Review Group Expectations: Print a copy of the Group Expectations. Review the expectations together with the students and answer questions as they arise. Collaborate with your group to determine whether you need to modify or add expectations.

Assessment: Before proceeding, read the pre-group assessment instructions aloud to the students and have each student complete the form. Carefully examine the completed forms to verify that all questions have been answered.

Group Conclusion: Ask each student to share how they are feeling about being part of the group. Students may share with their partners or the group.

Scaling Fist to Five: Ask students to reflect on today's session. Using their hands, ask them to put up the number that represents how they are feeling

- 0 (fist): I feel totally overwhelmed and scared.
- 3: I feel okay, a little nervous but also excited.
- 5: I feel confident and enthusiastic.

Note to Facilitators: You can customize the material to fit the needs of your group. If your students are not yet readers, you can read the "Would You Rather?" game questions aloud and have students move to different sides of the room to show their answers. If you're working with students who are quiet or take time to feel comfortable, consider having them write their responses instead of sharing out loud, or break into smaller teams for discussion. Depending on your schedule, you can include as many or as few of the suggested activities as you'd like, add extra elements such as games or read-alouds, or skip certain parts to fit your time constraints better. Remember, the workbook is just the framework—you bring it to life.

EXECUTIVE FUNCTION GROUP EXPECTATIONS

BE A MINDFUL LISTENER

Listen from your heart. When others are speaking, we all must do our best to focus on what others say with all our senses, refrain from interrupting, and keep our minds in the present without trying to decide what we will say next.

ACTIVELY PARTICIPATE

We are here to work together, so it is important that each one of us is doing our part to participate and engage. This will help us deepen our understanding of the topic, ourselves, and one another. When we fully dive into listening and participating, we will get more out of the group and grow stronger emotionally.

SHOW KINDNESS TO YOURSELF AND OTHERS

It is okay to disagree, but we won't yell or call each other names. We can support each other in keeping the space safe. This means we respond with curiosity, not criticism. We work hard to repair and restore our relationships if there is a conflict or disagreement.

BE WILLING TO LEARN AND GROW

In our group, we will create a safe space to share, make mistakes, and learn from each other.

WHAT IS SAID IN HERE, STAYS IN HERE

In our group, we will keep what we talk about confidential. Confidentiality means keeping what is said in the group private and not discussing it outside of the group. We know that some things are private, and not everyone needs to know about them. However, because we are a group, we can't promise that everyone will keep what you say private. If you share that you plan to hurt yourself or someone else or that someone is hurting you, I will keep you safe, but telling someone who needs to know can help keep you and others safe as well.

CREATE YOUR OWN

30-MINUTE GROUPS: EXECUTIVE FUNCTION

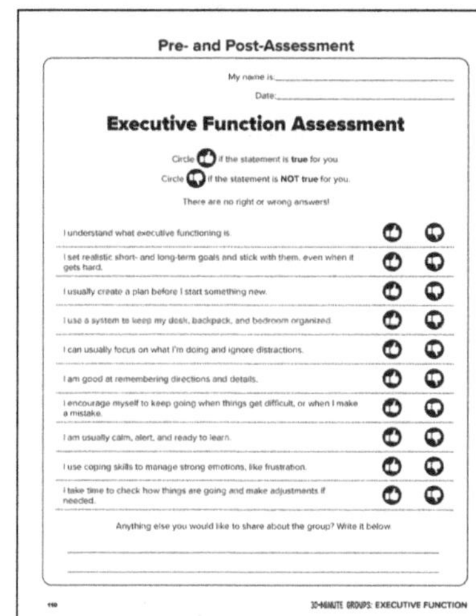

Pre- and Post-Assessment

My name is:

Date:

Executive Function Assessment

Circle [thumbs up] if the statement is **true** for you

Circle [thumbs down] if the statement is **NOT true** for you.

There are no right or wrong answers!

- I understand what executive functioning is.
- I set realistic short- and long-term goals and stick with them, even when it gets hard.
- I usually create a plan before I start something new.
- I use a system to keep my desk, backpack, and bedroom organized.
- I can usually focus on what I'm doing and ignore distractions.
- I am good at remembering directions and details.
- I encourage myself to keep going when things get difficult, or when I make a mistake.
- I am usually calm, alert, and ready to learn.
- I use coping skills to manage strong emotions, like frustration.
- I take time to check how things are going and make adjustments if needed.

Anything else you would like to share about the group? Write it below.

30-MINUTE GROUPS: EXECUTIVE FUNCTION

CHAPTER 1

WHAT IS EXECUTIVE FUNCTION?

MIND MAP

On the board, draw a Mind Map and ask students to consider the meaning of *Executive Function*. Ask them to also brainstorm different areas in their life where they can set goals or work on improving.

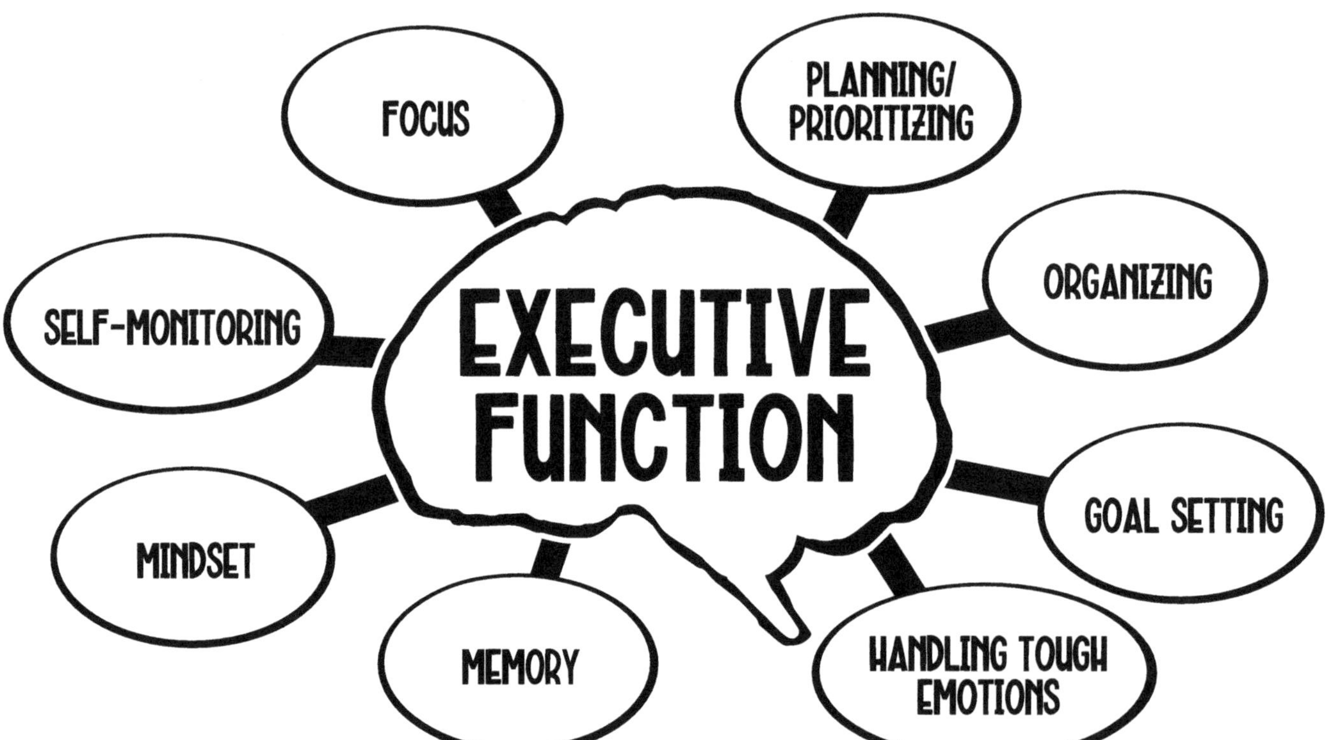

ASCA® STANDARDS

- **M 1.** Belief in development of whole self, including a healthy balance of mental, social/emotional, and physical well-being
- **M 3.** Positive attitude toward work and learning
- **B-LS 4.** Self-motivation and self-direction for learning

DIRECTIONS

- Begin the group by asking members to share a **Peak** and **Pit** from their week.

Share a positive or high moment from the week. Something that made you smile or feel good.

Share a low from the week. How did you get through it?

Alternatively, students can use an emotion scale to rate their feelings on a scale of 1 (not feeling great) to 10 (feeling their best).

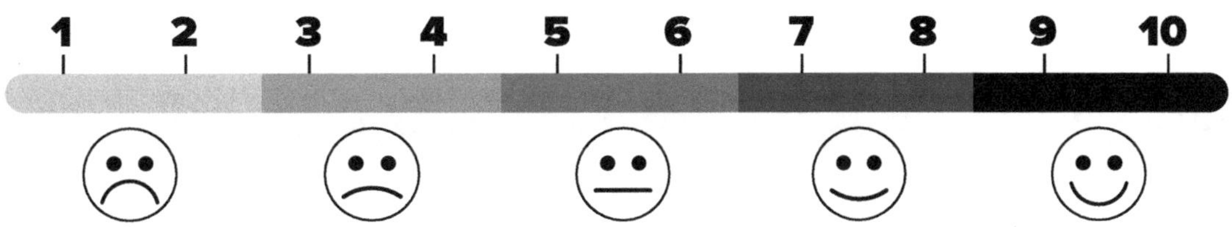

- Review the Group Expectations.
- Read the Lesson Introduction and ask the Circle Time Questions before reading the Story and asking the Discussion Questions. Students can share individually or turn and talk to share their answers in pairs.
- Complete one of the Skill Practice Activities. If time allows, complete the Would You Rather? cards (in a group or pairs) and any of the Additional Activities.
- Be sure to complete the Closing Considerations with each lesson.

LESSON INTRODUCTION

When you hear the word "skills" you might think about skills like being able to dribble a basketball or being a talented artist who can paint. But did you know there are other skills, skills that will help us both now and as we get older? These skills help us succeed in school and will help us when we get a job.

These skills are called executive functioning (EF) skills. EF skills help us get things done. They help us stay on task, keep organized, and regulate our emotions.

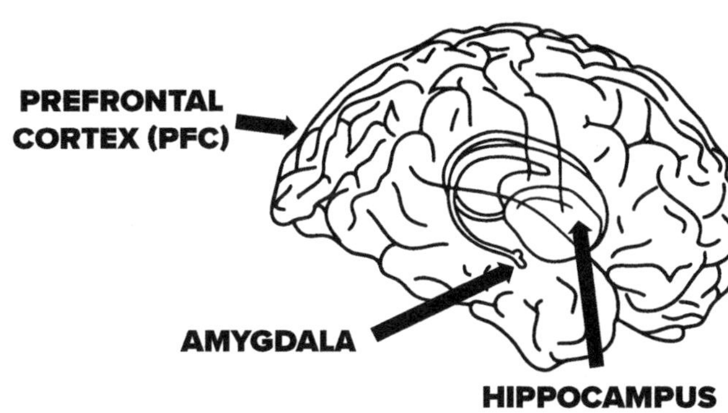

Skills like handling strong feelings (self-regulation), thinking positively, planning ahead, setting goals, organizing materials, remembering information, and staying focused are all executive functioning (EF) skills. These skills happen in the front part of our brain, called the **Prefrontal Cortex (PFC).**

The PFC is like a thoughtful turtle or wise owl that helps us think before we act and make decisions we are proud of.

There are two other important parts of the brain you should know about:

- The **amygdala** is a tiny, almond-shaped part of the brain that feels and responds to our emotions. It's like a guard dog that keeps us safe.
  When we face challenges like a hard test or experience a strong emotion like disappointment, our amygdala might mistake the feeling as a danger and react. This can lead to us doing or saying things we regret.
- The **hippocampus** helps us remember. This is our memory-saver. It helps us learn and remember new things. It also allows us to recall things we have learned in the past.
  Just as we can work out to build stronger muscles, we can also do things to help "train our brains." In our group we are going to help build our EF skills and strengthen our PFC.

CIRCLE TIME QUESTIONS

Ask students to reflect and share their answers to the following questions with the group. Larger groups may need to be broken into smaller groups to give students ample time to share their answers and deepen the conversation.

Use the Mind Map for reference.

- Which skill do you think is your strongest?
- Which skill do you think you need the most help with?
- Which skill are you the most curious about?
- Why do you think you need these skills?

STORY TIME

Hand out the Coloring Sheets and crayons or markers to younger students while the facilitator reads the story, if desired.

Brooklyn's Ruff Day

Brooklyn the puppy was so excited for her first day of puppy school! She jumped out of bed, wagging her tail, and ran straight to the door—knocking over her water bowl with a big splash. While she was cleaning it up, she got distracted by the puddles and started splashing around. "This is so fun!" she thought.

Suddenly, she heard her mom call, "Brooklyn, it's time to go!" Uh-oh! Brooklyn raced around looking for her leash and treats, but her bed was a tangled mess of toys, blankets, and chewed socks. By the time she found what she needed, she was already late. When she got to puppy school, she realized she had missed the morning games and felt grumpy. "What a ruff morning," Brooklyn thought.

Just then, her Doberman friend, Bindu, wandered over. "Are you ready for the sit-and-stay test?" he asked. "What test?" Brooklyn yelped. She had completely forgotten about it! She remembered telling herself weeks ago to practice every day, but she never did. Now it was test day, and she wasn't prepared. She felt so upset that she started to cry and told Bindu all about her terrible morning.

"Don't worry, Brooklyn," Bindu said gently. "There are special skills that can help you remember, plan ahead, and stay organized. They're called executive functioning skills. Think of them like 'sit' and 'stay' commands for your brain. If you want, I can help you practice them."

So, each week, they worked on a different skill, like keeping track of time, making checklists, and staying focused. Six weeks later, Brooklyn had learned how to manage her time, remember important tasks, and keep her things in order. She felt so proud on the day she earned her Good Canine Citizen award. "Now I'm ready for anything!" she barked happily.

DISCUSSION QUESTIONS

- What feelings did you hear in the story?
- What do you think Brooklyn could have done differently to get ready for school?
- What EF skills do you think Brooklyn needs help with (refer to Mind Map if needed)?
- What do you think Brooklyn could do next?
- What advice would you give Brooklyn?

SKILL PRACTICE

Give each student a piece of paper and some coloring supplies. Ask them to think quietly about a time when they felt frustrated because something went wrong—like when they lost something important or forgot their homework at home.

Next, have them draw a picture of that memory. Afterward, ask them to reflect: *Was there something I could have done to prevent that outcome? What skills would have helped me in this situation?* If they have an idea, they can draw a second picture showing what they could have done differently and how it might have changed the outcome.

Allow quiet time for drawing and reflection. Afterward, invite students to share their ideas if they feel comfortable.

Ask students to think about the memory they just recalled and identify which parts of their brain were involved:

- Which part helped you remember the experience? (Hippocampus)
- Which part felt the frustration or strong emotion? (Amygdala)
- Which part helped you reflect and think about how you could have responded differently? (Prefrontal Cortex or PFC)

ADDITIONAL ACTIVITIES

ELEMENTARY

MY BRAIN

Share these scenarios. Ask students to point to the part of the brain on their coloring sheet or call out the part of the brain that helps with this activity.

- You read a book and when a friend asks you about it you can tell them all about it. (hippocampus)
- Your teacher gives you a big project and you make a plan to do a little each day so you're ready. (PFC).
- You get to a hard question on a test and throw your pencil on the floor. (amygdala)
- You clean your backpack so it's ready for school on Monday (PFC).
- You learn a new idea. (PFC).

MIDDLE/HIGH

IDENTIFYING SKILLS

Share this scenario with the students and ask which executive function (EF) skills could have helped:

Imagine this: You get a big project that's due in two weeks. Since it seems like you have plenty of time, you decide to wait a week before starting. When the week is up, you sit down to begin—but you can't find the materials you need. Frustrated, you give up and start watching videos instead. The next day, you try again, but phone notifications keep distracting you. The following day, you finally start the project, but it turns out to be more complicated than you expected. Overwhelmed and frustrated, you just want to give up.

- Focus
- Planning/Prioritizing
- Organizing
- Goal setting
- Handling tough emotions (or self-regulating)
- Memory
- Mindset
- Self-Monitoring

CLOSING CONSIDERATIONS

Today we talked about three parts of our brain: our Prefrontal Cortex, Amygdala, and Hippocampus. Executive function skills happen in the front part of our brain, called the Prefrontal Cortex (PFC). Skills like handling strong feelings (self-regulation), thinking positively, planning ahead, setting goals, organizing materials, remembering information, and staying focused are all executive functioning (EF) skills.

Scaling Fist to Five

Ask students to reflect on today's session. Using their hands, ask them to put up the number that represents how they are feeling

- **0 (fist):** I feel totally overwhelmed and confused. I need lots of help.
- **3:** I understand it, but I need some support and practice.
- **5:** I feel confident. I could teach someone else all about this and how to do it.

"WOULD YOU RATHER?" GAME

Playing the "Would You Rather?" the game is a fun and engaging activity for students to develop their critical thinking skills. Students will reflect on their experience, evaluate their options based on their preferences, and reflect on the opinions of others, which provides different perspectives and strengthens the group's sense of connection to one another.

WOULD YOU RATHER?

Review cards before playing and remove any that may not be relevant or developmentally appropriate for your students. Copy and cut out the questions for small groups to discuss. You can also have students sit/stand or have each person stand in the center of the room and move toward one side or the other to show their vote for either option as the facilitator reads the questions aloud.

HAVE AMAZING PLANNING SKILLS OR STAY CALM UNDER PRESSURE?	BE REALLY GOOD AT MANAGING YOUR TIME OR HAVE A GREAT MEMORY?
BE ABLE TO PLAN EVERY TASK PERFECTLY OR ADAPT TO ANY CHANGE RIGHT AWAY?	NEVER GET DISTRACTED OR ACHIEVE A GOAL?
LEARN ABOUT A NEW IDEA BY WATCHING A VIDEO OR READING ABOUT IT?	HAVE A SUPER MEMORY OR UNSTOPPABLE FOCUS?

OUR BRAIN!

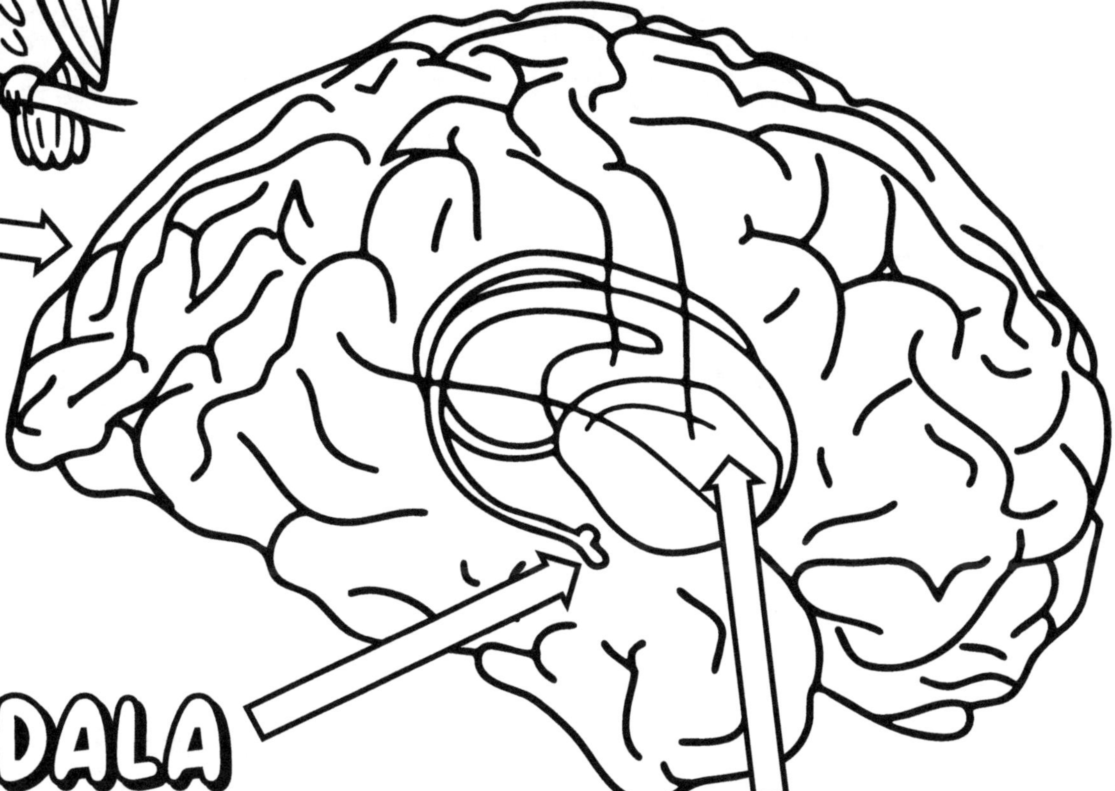

PFC

The pre-frontal cortex helps us make wise and thoughtful decisions. It helps us think before we act, solve problems, and set goals.

AMYGDALA

The amygdala is our "guard dog." It is always trying to sense danger and keep us safe.

HIPPOCAMPUS

The hippocampus is our memory saver. It helps you remember things you've learned and experiences.

CHAPTER 2

Setting Goals

MIND MAP

ELEMENTARY

On the board, draw a Mind Map and ask students to consider the meaning of *Goals*. Ask them to also brainstorm different areas in their lives where they can set goals or work on improving.

MIDDLE/HIGH

On the board, draw a Mind Map and ask students to consider the meaning of *Smart Goals.*

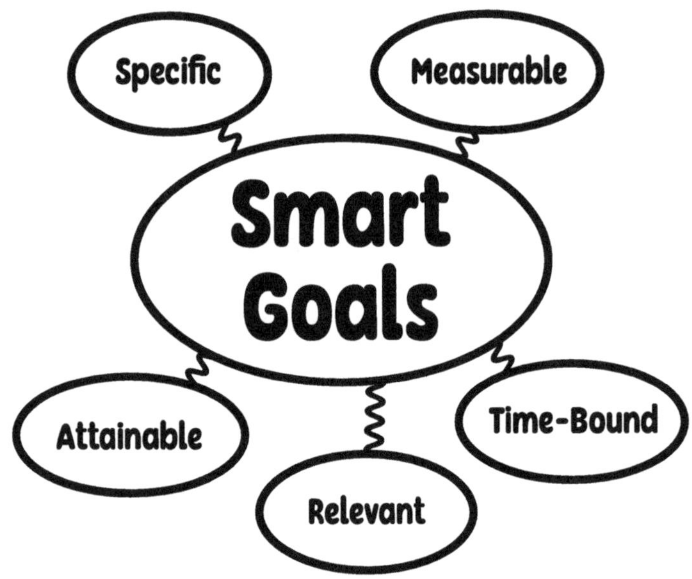

ASCA® STANDARDS

- **B-LS 4.** Self-motivation and self-direction for learning
- **B-LS 7**. Long- and short-term academic, career, and social/emotional goals
- **B-SMS 5.** Perseverance to achieve long and short-term goals

DIRECTIONS

- Begin the group by asking members to share a **Peak** and **Pit** from their week.

Share a positive or high moment from the week. Something that made you smile or feel good.

Share a low from the week. How did you get through it?

Alternatively, students can use an emotion scale to rate their feelings on a scale of 1 (not feeling great) to 10 (feeling their best).

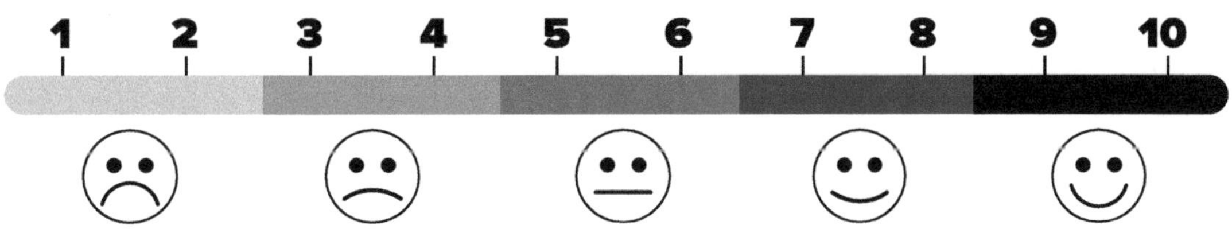

- Review the Group Expectations.
- Read the Lesson Introduction and ask the Circle Time Questions before reading the Story and asking the Discussion Questions. Students can share individually or turn and talk to share their answers in pairs.
- Complete one of the Skill Practice Activities. If time allows, complete the Would You Rather? cards (in a group or pairs) and any of the Additional Activities.
- Be sure to complete the Closing Considerations with each lesson.

LESSON INTRODUCTION

This week, we will focus on the skill of goal setting.

Setting goals is an important skill that helps our brain plan, stay organized, and get things done. When we set a goal, it gives us a clear path to follow and helps us use our thinking skills to reach it! Our prefrontal cortex helps us set goals.

Setting goals is also a powerful skill that taps into several key executive function abilities. When we set a goal, we decide on something important we want to achieve, and that decision helps our brain get organized. To reach that goal, we use skills like planning, organizing, and staying focused—skills that are all part of executive function. For example, goal setting helps us break down big tasks into smaller, manageable steps. This uses our planning and organization skills, which allow us to stay on track and make progress. Executive function skills also help us stay focused on our goal, which requires attention and concentration.

By the end of our group lesson today, I would like you to set a personal goal you want to achieve during our time together. This goal can be related to your interests, such as making the soccer team, or it can be about school, like earning A's and B's on your next report card.

It's important that our goals are realistic and attainable—something you can accomplish within the next 1–2 months. For instance, saying, "I want to read all the books in the library," is unrealistic, but setting a goal to read for thirty minutes each week is much more achievable.

CIRCLE TIME QUESTIONS

Ask students to reflect upon and share their answers to the following questions with the group. Larger groups may need to be broken into smaller groups to give students ample time to share their answers and deepen the conversation.

- Why do you think setting goals is important?
- What might stop someone from reaching a goal?
- Tell us about a time you succeeded at something, even when it got hard.
- What skills and strengths do you have that help you reach your goals?

STORY TIME

Hand out the Coloring Sheets and crayons or markers to younger students while the facilitator reads the story, if desired.

Laura's Big Library Goal

The first time Laura walked into the public library, she couldn't believe her eyes—there were rows and rows of books everywhere! She looked around, wide-eyed, spotting some of her favorites: *The Babysitters Club, Nancy Drew, Goosebumps.* It was like a dream!

She sat on the floor, surrounded by books, and made a big decision. "I'm going to read them ALL by the end of the year!" she thought. It was already March, but if she read every single day, she could do it!

Excited, she grabbed as many books as she could carry and marched to the checkout desk. But the librarian smiled and said, "Sorry, you can only check out three at a time."

"Oh no!" Laura thought. But she quickly came up with a new plan. "If I check out three books every week, I can still read the whole *Nancy Drew* series!"

The first week, she read all three books and rushed back for more. The next week, she only finished two. "Uh-oh," she thought. "I'll just have to read all day Saturday—maybe even skip lunch!"

But when lunchtime came, her stomach growled. Just then, her friends called, "Come outside and take a walk with us!"

"I want to, but I have to read," Laura sighed.

"Why? Do we have a project due?" one friend asked.

"No," Laura groaned and explained her goal.

Her friends looked at her with big eyes. "Laura, you're the biggest reader we know, but that sounds impossible! What if you read for just one hour a week?"

Laura thought about it. That actually sounded like a goal she could reach! She decided to read for fifteen minutes after school each day. That way, she could enjoy her books *and* still have time for other kinds of fun.

By the end of the year, Laura hadn't read *every* book in the library—but she had read so many amazing stories that she started writing her own!

DISCUSSION QUESTIONS

- What was Laura's goal? Was it realistic?
- What obstacles did Laura encounter while trying to reach her reading goal?
- Why did Laura change her original goal, and how did she make it more achievable?
- How did Laura's friends help her think differently about her reading goal?
- What advice would you have given Laura?

SKILL PRACTICE

Read the example goals to students:

- By May, I will memorize at least one song for the chorus auditions by practicing the lyrics for ten minutes each day and testing myself once a week to see if I can sing it from memory.
- I will earn an A on my next two social studies tests by completing my homework every day and studying for at least twenty minutes each night.
- I will improve my math grade from a B to an A by the end of the semester by completing all my homework on time, reviewing notes for twenty minutes each night, and asking my teacher for help when needed.
- I will make the dance team by practicing for thirty minutes every day, attending all tryout prep sessions, and asking a current team member for tips before tryouts in April.

Ask students what they noticed about the goals. For example, that they followed the SMART format or that they are realistic and included a deadline.

Pass out to students with the **Goal-Setting Road Map Activity Sheet** included at the end of this chapter and writing materials.

Ask students to think about a goal they can realistically accomplish within the next one or two months. Ask them to write down their goal where it says "final destination" on their road map.

Now, tell students to go back to the starting point of their map. Think about the journey ahead—what key steps or stops will they need to take to reach your goal? Write them down in order at each **Checkpoint**.

Next, ask them to think about what obstacles or setbacks might slow them down. Consider possible challenges. Have them write down their ideas near the **Roadblocks & Detours** icon.

Last, have them write about **Fuel & Pit Stops** that will help along the way. What tools, strategies, or support will keep them moving forward? Think about resources, motivation, or people who can help along the way.

With partners or in a group, have students share their goals and maps.

ADDITIONAL ACTIVITIES

ELEMENTARY MIDDLE/HIGH

GUIDED IMAGERY: YOUR JOURNEY TO SUCCESS

Close your eyes or look softly at a spot in front of you. Take a deep breath in, and as you let it out, imagine you are getting ready for a really important adventure. What's the big goal you're aiming for?

Before you start, think about what you need to take with you—not clothes or snacks, but the skills, knowledge, and strengths that will help you on your journey. Picture yourself packing these things into a suitcase, one by one. What would you include? Now, think about who will join you on this trip. Who is cheering you on? A teacher, a friend, or a family member? Imagine them walking next to you and encouraging you every step of the way.

As you begin your adventure, you arrive at your first stop—the Confidence Boost Stop. Here, there are people cheering for you! Listen to their encouraging words and feel their support. Look around—what do you see? What are you doing? How does it feel to be supported like this? After enjoying the cheers, you wave goodbye and continue on your path.

As you move forward, you see signs that help you know you're going in the right direction. Soon, you reach another important stop—the First Step Stop. Here, you take your first action toward your goal. What are you doing? How does it feel to finally start? What thoughts pop into your mind?

Keep going on your adventure, making as many stops as you need. Maybe you'll find a Problem-Solving Stop where you figure something out or a Growth Stop where you learn something new. Each stop brings you closer to reaching your goal.

Now, in the distance, you see it—your Finish Line! You've made it! Picture yourself celebrating your success. What are you doing? What do you see all around you? How do you feel right now? Take a deep breath in, and as you breathe out, bring your attention back to the present. When you're ready, open your eyes and carry this amazing vision with you as you move forward!

MIDDLE/HIGH

SMART GOAL PRACTICE

Write the SMART goal acronym on the board:

- **S**pecific
- **M**easurable
- **A**ttainable
- **R**elevant
- **T**ime-bound

I Do: Give students an example of a goal with all these components. For example, *SMART Goal for Reading:*

- **S (Specific):** I will read for one hour each week by reading for fifteen minutes after school every day.
- **M (Measurable):** I will track my reading time in a journal to make sure I reach one hour each week.
- **A (Achievable):** I can fit fifteen minutes of reading into my daily routine without missing out on other activities.
- **R (Relevant):** Reading more will help me enjoy new stories, improve my skills, and reach my goal of finishing more books.
- **T (Time-bound):** I will follow this plan for the next three months and adjust if needed to stay on track.

We Do: Ask students to work together to come up with a goal for their group. For example, *SMART Goal for a Counseling Small Group (Talking & Listening to Others):*

- **S (Specific):** I will practice talking and listening in my small group by sharing at least one thought and responding to a friend each session.
- **M (Measurable):** I will keep track by marking a check each time I share and listen during a group.
- **A (Achievable):** I will start by saying short answers and get more comfortable sharing over time.
- **R (Relevant):** Talking and listening will help me make friends, share my ideas, and feel more confident.
- **T (Time-bound):** I will work on this for the next six group meetings and check in on how I'm doing.

You Do: Have students create their own SMART goal they wish to accomplish during the course of the group.

CLOSING CONSIDERATIONS

Setting goals is like giving your brain a roadmap. When you know exactly what you want to achieve, it's easier to plan your steps, stay organized, and follow through. That's where executive function comes in—it's the set of skills in the front part of your brain (the Prefrontal Cortex or PFC) that helps you think things through, stay focused, and manage your time and emotions.

Scaling Fist to Five

Ask students to reflect on today's session. Using their hands, ask them to put up the number that represents how they are feeling

- **0 (fist):** I feel totally overwhelmed and confused. I need lots of help.
- **3:** I understand it, but I need some support and practice.
- **5:** I feel confident. I could teach someone else all about this and how to do it.

"WOULD YOU RATHER?" GAME

Playing the "Would You Rather?" the game is a fun and engaging activity for students to develop their critical thinking skills. Students will reflect on their experience, evaluate their options based on their preferences, and reflect on the opinions of others, which provides different perspectives and strengthens the group's sense of connection to one another.

Would You Rather?

Review cards before playing and remove any that may not be relevant or developmentally appropriate for your students. Copy and cut out the questions for small groups to discuss. You can also have students sit/stand or have each person stand in the center of the room and move toward one side or the other to show their vote for either option as the facilitator reads the questions aloud.

FOCUS ON ONE GOAL AT A TIME OR WORK ON SEVERAL GOALS ALL AT ONCE?	HAVE A CAREGIVER OR TEACHER CHEERING YOU ON WHILE YOU WORK TOWARD YOUR GOAL, OR HAVE A FRIEND CHEERING YOU ON ALONG THE WAY?
CELEBRATE REACHING YOUR GOAL WITH LOTS OF CHEERS AND KIND WORDS FROM EVERYONE, OR WITH A SPECIAL GIFT FROM YOUR FRIENDS AND FAMILY?	TELL SOMEONE ABOUT YOUR GOAL OR PRIVATELY WRITE IT DOWN?
SET A BIG, EXCITING GOAL THAT TAKES A LONG TIME TO ACHIEVE OR A SMALL, EASY GOAL THAT YOU CAN ACCOMPLISH QUICKLY?	ACHIEVE YOUR GOAL, BUT NOBODY KNOWS ABOUT IT, OR ALMOST REACH YOUR GOAL BUT EVERYONE CELEBRATES YOUR EFFORT?

G.P.S.

GOALS•PLAN•SUCCESS

"Begin with the end in mind."

STEPHEN COVEY

Goal-Setting Road Map

1. **Final Destination**
   Think about a realistic goal for the next 1-2 months and write it here.
2. **Checkpoints**
   List the steps needed to accomplish your goal in order. Note: Some steps may require multiple substeps.
3. **Roadblocks & Detours**
   List any challenges you might face.

   Fuel & Pit Stops
   List resources or support that will help you stay on track.

CHECKPOINT
Steps/Mini Goals

ROADBLOCKS & DETOURS
Obstacles or Setbacks

FUEL & PIT STOPS
Tools, Strategies, and Support

START

FINAL DESTINATION

CHAPTER 3

Planning/Prioritizing

MIND MAP

ELEMENTARY

On the board, draw a Mind Map, and ask students to consider the meaning of *Plan*. Use words that are developmentally appropriate for your students.

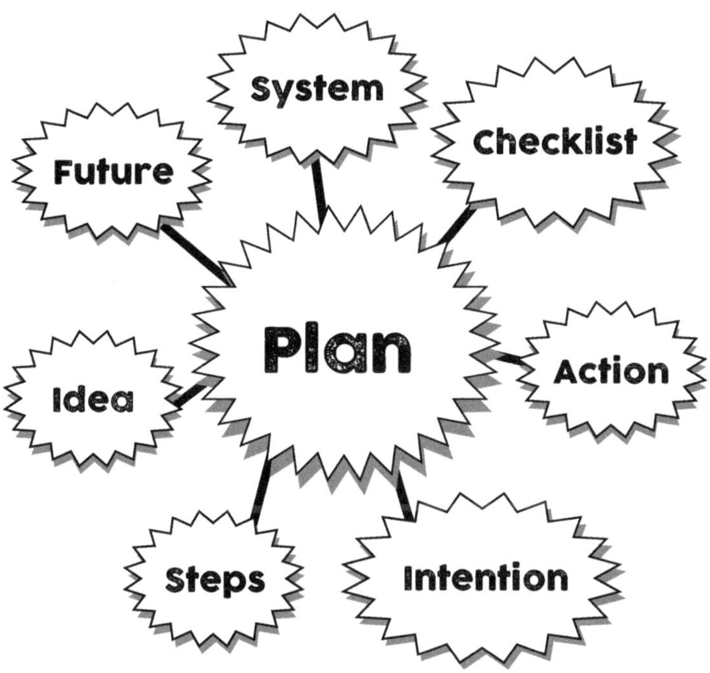

MIDDLE/HIGH

On the board, draw a Mind Map, and write the word *Prefrontal Cortex*. The prefrontal cortex (PFC) helps us plan and make wise and thoughtful decisions. It's the part of the brain that helps us think before we act or speak. The PFC also allows us to regulate our emotions and behaviors.

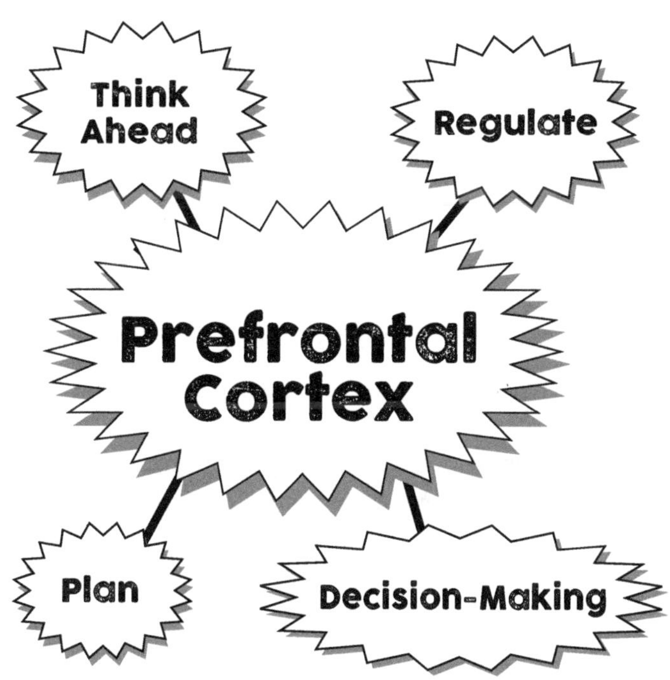

ASCA® STANDARDS

- **B-LS 4.** Self-motivation and self-direction for learning
- **B-LS 3.** Time management, organizational and study skills
- **B-LS 1**. Critical thinking skills to make informed decisions

DIRECTIONS

- Begin the group by asking members to share a **Peak** and **Pit** from their week.

Share a positive or high moment from the week. Something that made you smile or feel good.

Share a low from the week. How did you get through it?

Alternatively, students can use an emotion scale to rate their feelings on a scale of 1 (not feeling great) to 10 (feeling their best).

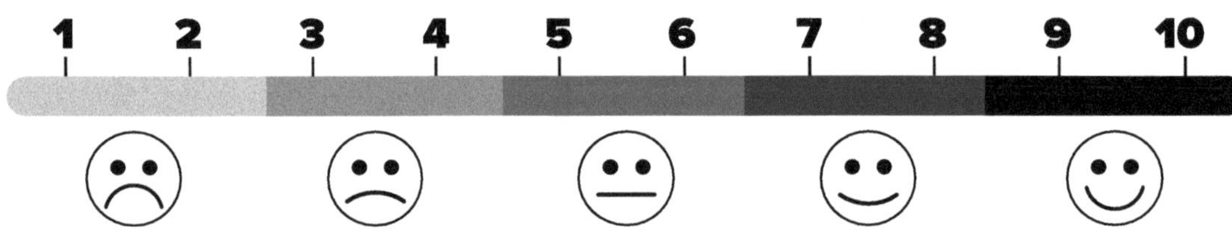

- Review the Group Expectations.
- Read the Lesson Introduction and ask the Circle Time Questions before reading the Story and asking the Discussion Questions. Students can share individually or turn and talk to share their answers in pairs.
- Complete one of the Skill Practice Activities. If time allows, complete the Would You Rather? cards (in a group or pairs) and any of the Additional Activities.
- Be sure to complete the Closing Considerations with each lesson.

LESSON INTRODUCTION

Last week, we set goals for ourselves. Today, let's use our rating scale to see how we're doing. Our scale goes from 1 to 10: 1 means "I haven't started, or it's been really hard" and 10 means "I reached my goal!"

Think about where you are on this scale. If you're at a 4, what could you do to move up to a 5? Maybe you could try a new idea, ask a friend or adult for help, or change your plan. If you're at a 10, ask yourself whether the goal was too easy. Could you try a bigger challenge next time?

Today we are going to talk about two EF skills that help us reach our goals: planning and prioritizing. Our PFC helps us plan and prioritize.

Planning means thinking ahead and making a list of what we need to do or what supplies we need. For example, if I have a big project, I might write down all the steps I need to take before I start.

Prioritizing means deciding which tasks are most important and doing those first. For example, if I need to get ready for school, brushing my teeth is more important than playing online. Using planning and prioritizing helps us stay on track, feel less stressed, and move us closer to our goals!

CIRCLE TIME QUESTIONS

Ask students to reflect and share their answers to the following questions with the group. Larger groups may need to be broken into smaller groups to give students ample time to share their answers and deepen the conversation.

ELEMENTARY

- How is a plan different from a goal?
- When you imagine yourself getting ready for school, what do you see?
- What materials and supplies (like backpack, lunch, etc.) do you need to get ready? How can you prepare the night before?
- What is the first thing you need to do or the most important thing you need to do to get ready for school?

MIDDLE/HIGH

- How is creating a plan different from setting a goal?
- When you picture yourself starting at a new school (getting ready to move to the next school building, middle school, high school, or college), how do you imagine preparing both practically and mentally?
- What steps can you take now to feel ready for this transition?
- Which step or task is the most important—or most urgent—to do first?

STORY TIME

Hand out the Coloring Sheets and crayons or markers to younger students while the facilitator reads the story, if desired.

Stan With a Plan

Stan really wanted to improve his grades this year. His grandmother had promised that if he got all A's and B's on his report card, he could get a puppy! Stan was sure he could do it—but there was one big problem... mornings!

Stan was not a morning person. Every day, when his grandfather said, "Time to get up," Stan would mumble, "Five more minutes," and then sleep for ten! Then, he'd rush around trying to find his missing shoe or his lost homework. By the time he got to school, he already felt behind.

Determined to get that puppy, Stan decided he needed a plan!

- He packed his backpack the night before and made a checklist to be sure he had everything ready.

- He set two alarms—one to wake up and one to remind him it was time to get out of bed for real!
- He even put a picture in the bathroom to remind himself of all the steps he needed to get ready.

Little by little, Stan's mornings got easier. He wasn't late. He didn't forget his homework. And best of all—his grades started going up!

At the end of the nine weeks, Stan did it! He had all A's and B's on his report card. And best of all? He finally got to celebrate with sloppy, happy kisses from his new puppy, Boss!

DISCUSSION QUESTIONS

- What was Stan's goal?
- What steps did Stan include in his plan to have better mornings and reach his goal?
- How did having a plan help Stan stay organized?
- Would you add anything to that plan?
- Do you have a morning routine? Tell us about it.

SKILL PRACTICE

OPTION 1: MY PLAN FOR SUCCESS

Pass out the **My Plan for Success Worksheet** and writing materials.

Ask students to imagine a project, assignment, or homework they need to complete for school. Examples include an art project, a potato book character, or a social studies presentation.

Have students visualize what their completed project will look like when it's ready to turn in.

Instruct students to draw a sketch of their finished project in the section labeled "The End."

Next, ask students to think about the steps they need to take to complete their assignment. Have them complete the sentence starters in "The Middle" section.

Encourage students to consider what materials they will need to be prepared (e.g., pencils, markers, books, notes). They should list these materials in the "Start" section.

Once the worksheet is complete, allow students to share their answers in a group or with partners.

OPTION 2: WHAT'S THE PRIORITY?

Provide students with two blank pieces of paper and writing materials. Ask the students to "brain dump" or write down everything they need to do, all their upcoming assignments including homework, projects, etc.

Now ask students to sort the list by putting an "!" next to everything that is urgent and a star "*" next to everything that is important.

Once complete, have them use their second sheet of paper to create a "to-do list" with no more than 5 items. Numbers 1–3 on their list should be those things they identified as urgent and numbers 4–5 should be the important items. Give students the opportunity to share their answers in a group or with partners.

ADDITIONAL ACTIVITIES

ELEMENTARY MIDDLE/HIGH

HABIT STACKING: BUILDING ROUTINES EASILY

Habit Stacking is a simple strategy from James Clear's book *Atomic Habits*[1]. It helps students create routines by adding a new habit to something they already do every day.

Explain to students what Habit Stacking is: *"Habit Stacking means adding a new habit to something you already do—like connecting two puzzle pieces that fit perfectly!"*

Next, model Habit Stacking for students with an example. For example, "After I hang up my backpack, I'll put my homework in the turn-in tray."

Encourage students to create examples using sentence starters:

- "After I ____, I will ____."
- "Before I ____, I will ____."

Have students come up with their own Habit Stacking examples and share with a partner or the group.

ELEMENTARY

PRIORITIZING EVERYDAY TASKS

Give students a sheet of paper and crayons or highlighters. Ask them to write down things they do daily or weekly. For example:

- Do homework
- Feed my pet fish
- Pack my backpack
- Play with friends online
- Brush my teeth
- Read a book

Now ask students to look at their list and use different colors of highlighters to rank their tasks:

- Green = Top priority (Very important)
- Yellow = Medium priority (Important, but not urgent)
- Pink = Low priority (Can wait or is just for fun)

Once complete, ask students to share their lists and how they prioritized each activity.

Group Activity Option: Instead of individual work, write tasks on the board as students brainstorm aloud. Then, as a class, discuss and decide which tasks are high, medium, or low priority.

MIDDLE/HIGH

MY CALENDAR/MY PRIORITIES

Pass out to students with the **Monthly Calendar Template** included at the end of this chapter and writing materials. Ask them to write down important dates, such as:

- Test dates
- Project deadlines
- Application due dates
- School events (days off, assemblies, etc.)

Now have students think about what they need to do to prepare for these dates. Examples include:

- Study for a test
- Buy materials for a project
- Print and submit an application
- Request a letter of recommendation

Tell students to add their tasks to a specific day. Remind them that planning in advance helps them stay on track.

Ask students to look over their calendars and highlight their tasks based on importance:

- Green = Top priority (Must do ASAP)
- Yellow = Medium priority (Important but not urgent)
- Pink = Low priority (Can wait or is optional)

CLOSING CONSIDERATIONS

Today we talked about planning for things we need to do. Plans can help us accomplish small things, like cleaning our room, or larger projects, like reaching a major goal. How can you use what we learned today in your day or week?

Remember that when we prioritize, we are trying to figure out what is the most important thing to do right now. What is one priority you have for the week?

Scaling Fist to Five

Ask students to reflect on today's session. Using their hands, ask them to put up the number that represents how they are feeling

- **0 (fist):** I feel totally overwhelmed and confused. I need lots of help.
- **3:** I understand it, but I need some support and practice.
- **5:** I feel confident. I could teach someone else all about this and how to do it.

"WOULD YOU RATHER?" GAME

Playing the "Would You Rather?" the game is a fun and engaging activity for students to develop their critical thinking skills. Students will reflect on their experience, evaluate their options based on their preferences, and reflect on the opinions of others, which provides different perspectives and strengthens the group's sense of connection to one another.

Would You Rather?

Review cards before playing and remove any that may not be relevant or developmentally appropriate for your students. Copy and cut out the questions for small groups to discuss. You can also have students sit/stand or have each person stand in the center of the room and move toward one side or the other to show their vote for either option as the facilitator reads the questions aloud.

CREATE A PLAN WITH OTHERS OR WORK ALONE TO MAKE YOUR PLAN?	USE A PAPER OR DIGITAL CALENDAR (LIKE ON YOUR PHONE)?
HAVE A ROUTINE THAT IS ALWAYS THE SAME OR ONE THAT ALWAYS CHANGES?	HAVE A WEEKEND WITH LOTS OF THINGS TO DO OR ONE WITH NOTHING PLANNED?
START WITH EASY TASKS TO BUILD MOMENTUM OR DO THE HARDEST TASK FIRST TO GET IT OVER WITH?	HAVE A CHECKLIST TO KEEP TRACK OF THINGS YOU NEED TO DO OR GET REMINDERS FROM A PERSON?

My Grand Plan

Step 1. ______________________________

Step 2. ______________________________

Step 3. ______________________________

"All big things come from small beginnings."

JAMES CLEAR

MY PLAN FOR SUCCESS

Planning for success begins with the end in mind.

Start at **The End (Step 1)**, work your way back up to **The Middle (Step 2)** and then finish at **The Start (Step 3)**. Follow the instructions to complete each step.

THE START

Make a list of the supplies you need to complete your assignment.

_______________ _______________

_______________ _______________

_______________ _______________

_______________ _______________

_______________ _______________

3

THE MIDDLE

Think about how you need to complete your assignment and finish the sentences.

First I will _______________

Then I will _______________

Next I will _______________

Last I will _______________

2

THE END

Draw a sketch of what your assignment will look like when it's done.

1

MONTHLY CALENDAR

GREEN = Top Priority • **YELLOW** = Medium Priority • **PINK** = Low Priority

CHAPTER 4

ORGANIZATION

MIND MAP

On the board, draw a Mind Map and ask students to consider the meaning of *Organized*.

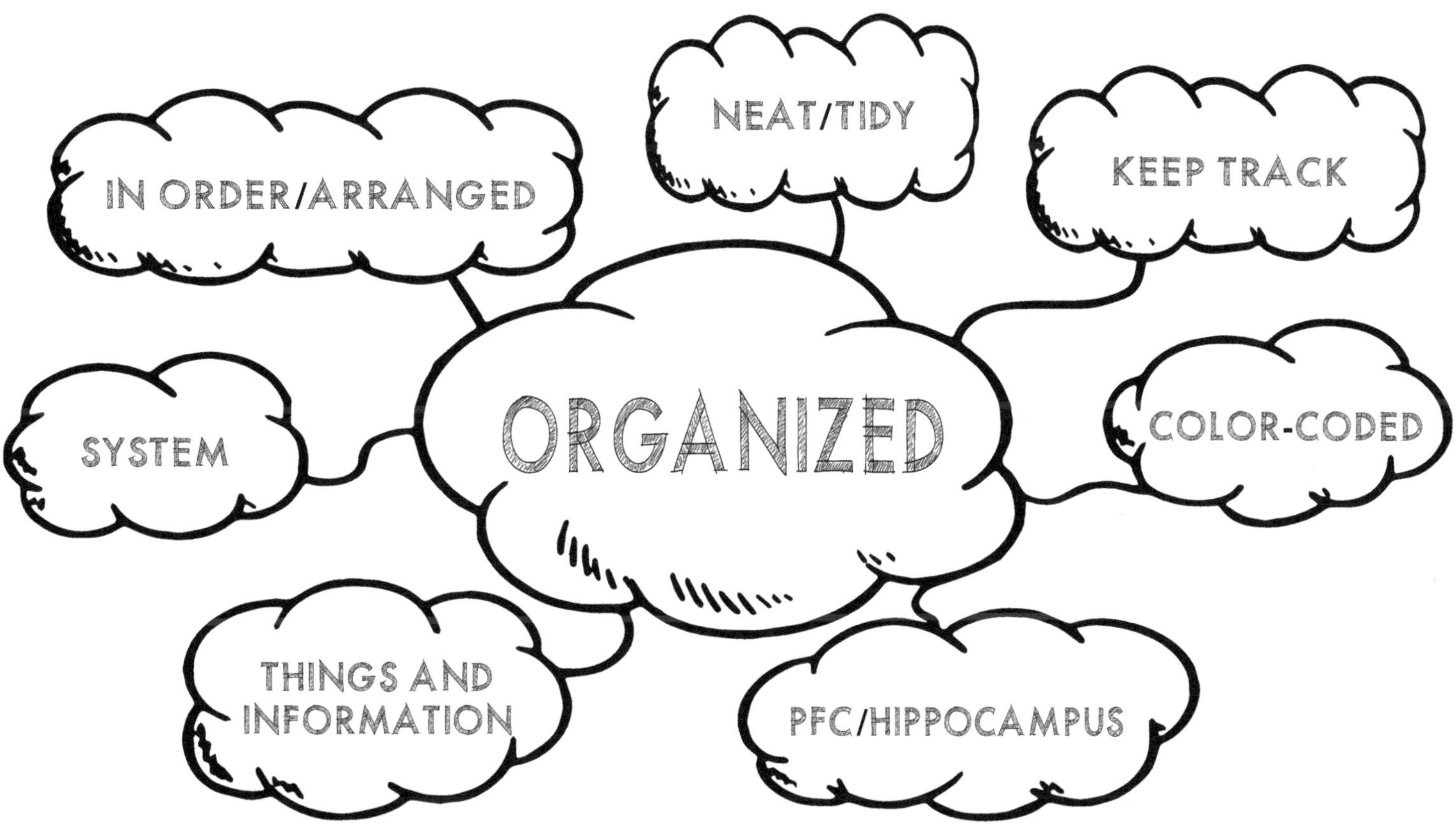

ASCA® STANDARDS

- **M 3.** Positive attitude toward work and learning
- **B-LS 3**. Time management, organizational, and study skills
- **B-SS 7**. Leadership and teamwork skills to work effectively in diverse groups

DIRECTIONS

- Begin the group by asking members to share a **Peak** and **Pit** from their week.

Share a positive or high moment from the week. Something that made you smile or feel good.

Share a low from the week. How did you get through it?

Alternatively, students can use an emotion scale to rate their feelings on a scale of 1 (not feeling great) to 10 (feeling their best).

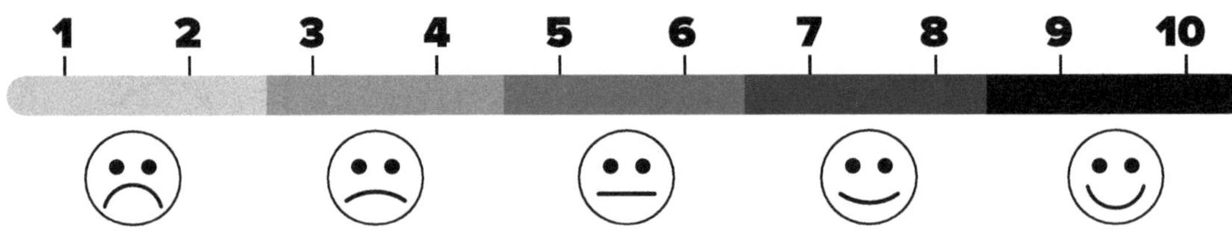

- Ask students to use the scale below to see how they're doing in reaching their goals. Our scale goes from 1 to 10: 1 means "I haven't started, or it's been really hard" and 10 means "I reached my goal!"

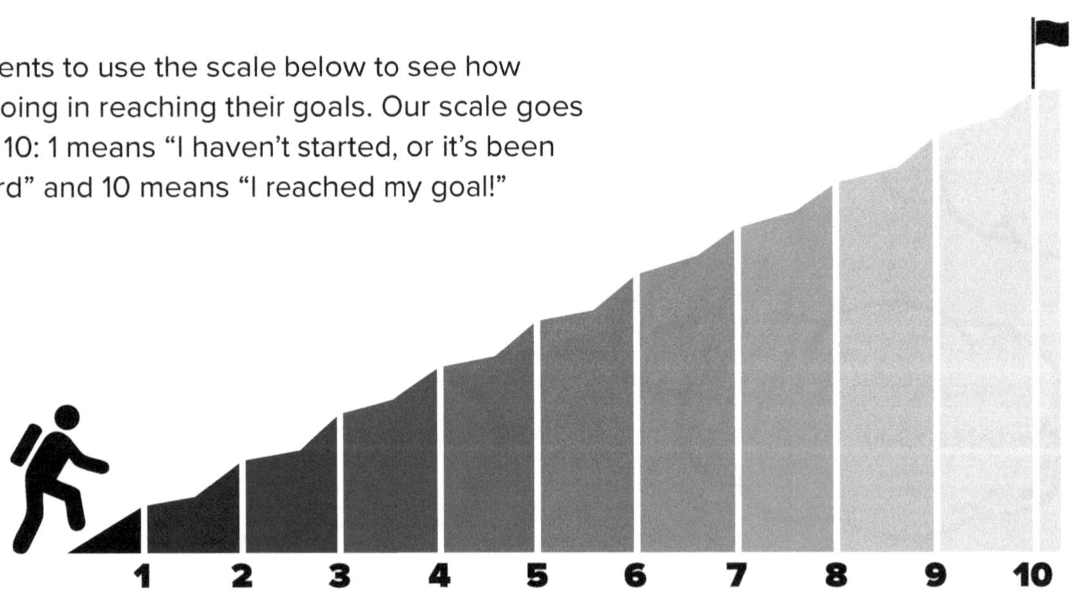

- Ask students to think about where they are on this scale and how they can move up? For example, if they're at a 4, what could they do to move up to a 5? Maybe they could try a new idea, ask a friend or adult for help, or change their plan. If they're at a 10, ask them to consider whether the goal was too easy. Could they try a bigger challenge next time?
- Review the Group Expectations.

- Read the Lesson Introduction and ask the Circle Time Questions before reading the Story and asking the Discussion Questions. Students can share individually or turn and talk to share their answers in pairs.
- Complete one of the Process Activities. If time allows, complete the Would You Rather cards (in a group or pairs) and Additional Activities.
- Be sure to complete the Closing Considerations with each lesson.

LESSON INTRODUCTION

We've learned that making plans helps us reach our goals and be successful each day. A big part of achieving our goals is having the right tools, supplies, and materials ready to go. Being organized makes it easier to find what we need when we need it. Our PFC helps us with the skill of making plans and setting goals, but it also helps us do something else.

Have you ever worked hard on your homework, only to feel frustrated when you couldn't find it later? Today, we're going to talk about how staying organized can help us save time, reduce stress, and stay on track!

CIRCLE TIME QUESTIONS

Ask students to reflect and share their answers to the following questions with the group. Larger groups may need to be broken into smaller groups to give students ample time to share their answers and deepen the conversation.

- Have you ever struggled with organization?
- Imagine your best friend asked for your advice on how to be organized. What would you say?
- What is the biggest roadblock to staying organized? What makes staying organized hard?

STORY TIME

Hand out the Coloring Sheets and crayons or markers to younger students while the facilitator reads the story, if desired.

Boss and the Case of the Missing Toy

> Boss loved toys. He had chew toys, snuggle toys, squeaky toys, and tug toys. He had so many toys, it was like living in a toy store, except messier. But Boss didn't mind one bit.
>
> His absolute favorite toy was Mr. Squeakers, a red rubber bone that made the perfect squeak. But there was one problem.
>
> Boss never put his toys away. They were everywhere: under the couch, on the stairs, in the laundry basket (don't ask). He figured if he could find Mr. Squeakers when he needed it, what was the big deal?

Then, one night at bedtime, disaster struck. Mr. Squeakers was missing.

"No! Where did you go?" Boss howled, searching everywhere: under the couch, behind the food bowl, and even in the laundry basket.

For a week, he worried. What if he never found Mr. Squeakers again?

One day, feeling defeated, Boss flopped onto the couch. SQUEAK!

His ears perked up. He sniffed around and pawed at the cushions. AHA! There was Mr. Squeakers, wedged between the cushions!

"BARK! YES! I found you!" Boss wagged his tail so hard he almost knocked over a lamp. He never wanted to lose Mr. Squeakers again.

He needed a plan. Boss got four big baskets and labeled them:

- Blue for chew toys.
- Green for tug toys.
- Yellow for special occasion toys.
- Purple for squeaky toys—including Mr. Squeakers!

Now, every time he finished playing, he put his toys in the right basket. Not only was the house cleaner, but he always knew where Mr. Squeakers was.

Everything was finally organized... until one day, Boss gasped. *"WAIT... Where's my favorite sock?!"* Oh no. Here we go again.

DISCUSSION QUESTIONS

- How did Boss change from the beginning to the end of the story? What did he start doing differently?
- What was Boss's new organization system, and how did it help him?
- Why was it a problem when Boss didn't have a system for his toys?
- Would you say you're more like Boss at the start of the story (messy) or at the end (organized)? Why?
- Have you ever lost something important? What could you do to keep track of your things like Boss did?

SKILL PRACTICE

Tell students you are challenging them to "beat the clock."

Have everyone **brainstorm different ways to categorize** schoolwork and materials. Some examples include:

- By Priority: Need to do immediately, To Do Soon, Complete
- By Action: Keep at home, Return to School, Trash
- By Subject: Social Studies, Science, Math, Reading

Allow students to choose the strategy that works best for them individually. If you're doing this activity with the whole class, have students vote on the organizational system they think will work best for them. They can vote by raising their hands or standing up.

Ask students to bring their backpacks to the group area. If you're doing this activity with the whole class, have students go to their desks or grab their backpacks.

Explain that they will now sort all their materials into their chosen categories. Set a timer for one to two minutes and challenge them to "beat the clock." Start the timer and let them organize until time is up.

Reflect & Discuss with partners or as a group discuss the following questions:

- How did they feel during the challenge?
- What did they notice about their desks or backpacks?
- What did they learn about organizing?
- How does this connect to staying organized in everyday life?
- Think back to our last lesson on planning and prioritizing. How can you include time for organizing in your plan or calendar? Where would you place organizing as a priority?

Bonus: Take a before and after picture of their desks so they can see their progress!

ADDITIONAL ACTIVITIES

ELEMENTARY

BACKPACK SCAVENGER HUNT

Before the activity, borrow a backpack (or multiple bags for different groups) and make it as messy as possible. Fill the bag with various items, such as:

- Pencil
- Crayon
- Paperclip
- A paper labeled "Social Studies Homework"
- A paper labeled "Keep at Home"
- Any other small items you'd like to include

Round 1: The Messy Search

Write the "hidden" objects on the board, give students a list, or have them write it down. Tell students their goal is to find all the objects as quickly as possible. Have them predict how long it will take. Start a stopwatch (or use your phone) and time how long it takes them to find everything.

Once they've found all the items, have them neatly organize the backpack. Discuss strategies for keeping a backpack tidy and why organization matters.

Round 2: The Organized Search

Tell students they will now repeat the scavenger hunt but with the organized backpack. Ask them to predict if they will be faster this time. Start the stopwatch again and time how long it takes.

Have students debrief on the activity. How did they feel during the game? What did they notice? Was it easier to find things with a messy or organized backpack? What did they learn? How does this relate to being organized?

MIDDLE/HIGH

LABEL MAKER

Ask students to list all the subjects or classes they are currently taking, such as Math, Science, Reading, and Social Studies. Then, have them choose a color to represent each subject. For example, Math might be blue, Science green, Reading red, and Social Studies yellow.

Once they have assigned colors, give them color dot stickers or Washi tape to label all the materials they need for each class. They can place a color dot on the spine of their textbooks, use Washi tape on folders, binders, or notebooks, and even mark pencil cases or storage pouches with the corresponding colors. This system will help them quickly find and organize their materials, making it easier to stay on top of their work.

CLOSING CONSIDERATIONS

Today we talked about staying organized. Being organized helps us have everything we need to accomplish our plans and reach our goals. Organization is a skill that helps us arrange our things in a way that makes them easy to find. It's an important EF skill.

Scaling Fist to Five

Ask students to reflect on today's session. Using their hands, ask them to put up the number that represents how they are feeling

- **0 (fist):** I feel totally overwhelmed and confused. I need lots of help.
- **3:** I understand it, but I need some support and practice.
- **5:** I feel confident. I could teach someone else all about this and how to do it.

"WOULD YOU RATHER?" GAME

Playing the "Would You Rather?" the game is a fun and engaging activity for students to develop their critical thinking skills. Students will reflect on their experience, evaluate their options based on their preferences, and reflect on the opinions of others, which provides different perspectives and strengthens the group's sense of connection to one another.

WOULD YOU RATHER?

Review cards before playing and remove any that may not be relevant or developmentally appropriate for your students. Copy and cut out the questions for small groups to discuss. You can also have students sit/stand or have each person stand in the center of the room and move toward one side or the other to show their vote for either option as the facilitator reads the questions aloud.

ORGANIZE BOOKS BY COLOR OR BY TITLE?	**HAVE ONE BINDER FOR EVERYTHING OR A SEPARATE BINDER FOR EACH SUBJECT?**
GET YOUR BACKPACK READY BEFORE BED OR FIRST THING IN THE MORNING?	**ORGANIZE YOUR THINGS BY YOURSELF OR WITH HELP FROM OTHERS?**
HAVE A LOCKER OR A SPACE IN EACH CLASSROOM TO KEEP YOUR MATERIALS?	**ORGANIZE A MESSY BEDROOM OR A MESSY DESK?**

Boss's Baskets

"For every minute spent in organizing, an hour is earned."

BENJAMIN FRANKLIN

CHAPTER 5

Focus

MIND MAP

ELEMENTARY

On the board, draw a Mind Map, and ask students to consider the meaning of *Whole Body Listening*.

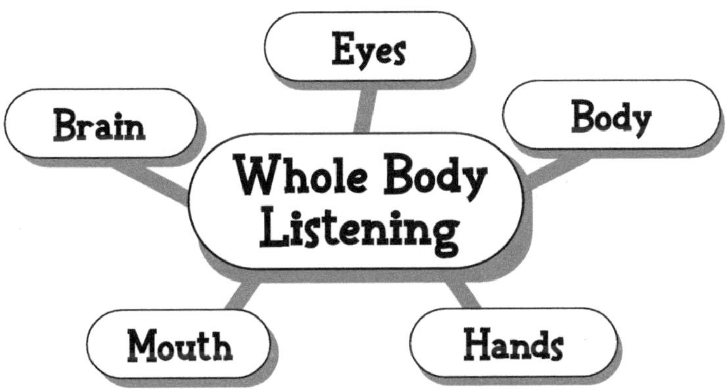

MIDDLE/HIGH

On the board, draw a Mind Map, and ask students to consider the meaning of *Active Listening*.

ASCA® STANDARDS

- **B-SMS 2.** Self-discipline and self-control
- **B-SS 1.** Effective oral and written communication skills and listening skills
- **B-SS 8.** Advocacy skills for self and others and ability to assert self, when necessary

DIRECTIONS

- Begin the group by asking members to share a **Peak** and **Pit** from their week.

Share a positive or high moment from the week. Something that made you smile or feel good.

Share a low from the week. How did you get through it?

Alternatively, students can use an emotion scale to rate their feelings on a scale of 1 (not feeling great) to 10 (feeling their best).

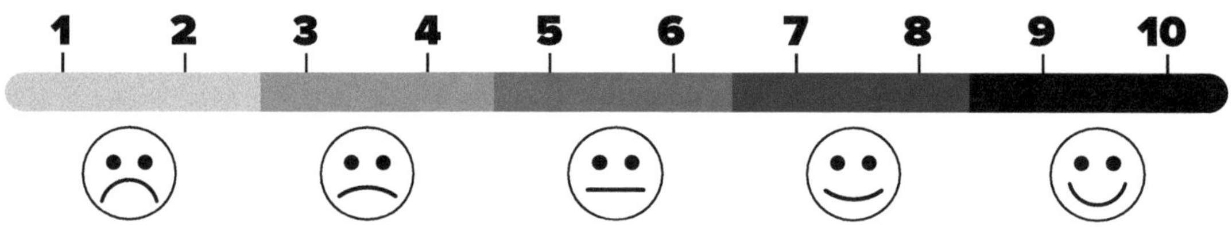

- Ask students to use the scale below to see how they're doing in reaching their goals. Our scale goes from 1 to 10: 1 means "I haven't started, or it's been really hard" and 10 means "I reached my goal!"

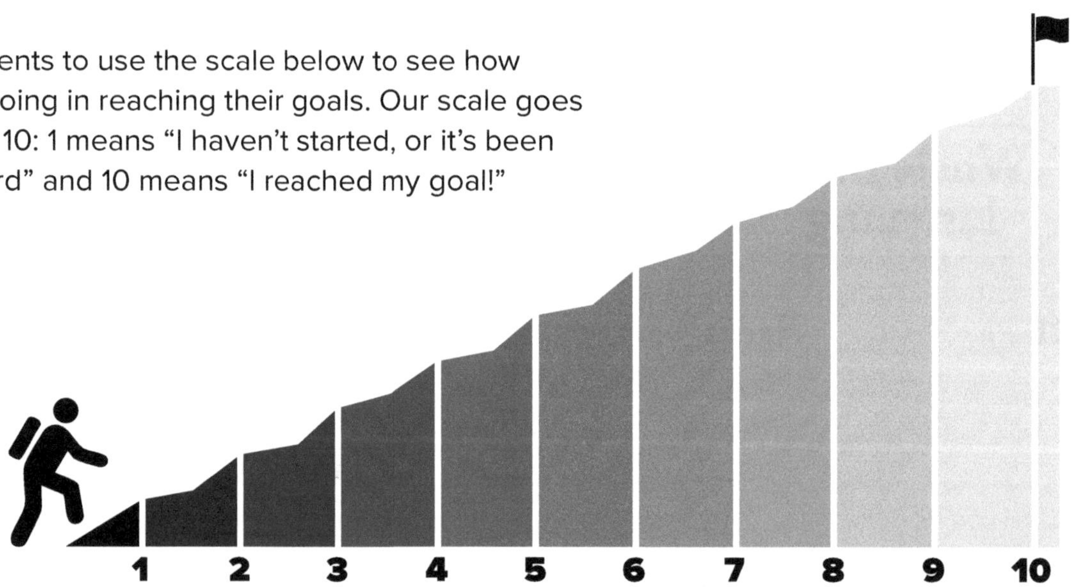

- Ask students to think about where they are on this scale and how they can move up? For example, if they're at a 4, what could they do to move up to a 5? Maybe they could try a new idea, ask a friend or adult for help, or change their plan. If they're at a 10, ask them to consider whether the goal was too easy. Could they try a bigger challenge next time?
- Review the Group Expectations.

- Read the Lesson Introduction and ask the Circle Time Questions before reading the Story and asking the Discussion Questions. Students can share individually or turn and talk to share their answers in pairs.
- Complete one of the Process Activities. If time allows, complete the Would You Rather cards (in a group or pairs) and Additional Activities.
- Be sure to complete the Closing Considerations with each lesson.

LESSON INTRODUCTION

Sometimes it can be hard to focus on what you are doing. Maybe you're in class and your best friend keeps talking to you while you're trying to work, or maybe you are trying to do your homework, but you keep thinking about something you watched online, or your phone keeps buzzing.

Today we are going to practice shifting our focus to the present and staying focused. Focusing on the present is a mindfulness skill that you can practice every day. It helps keep your amygdala calm and your PFC engaged.

CIRCLE TIME QUESTIONS

Ask students to reflect upon and share their answers to the following questions with the group. Larger groups may need to be broken into smaller groups to give students ample time to share their answers and deepen the conversation.

- What do good listeners DO or NOT DO?
- Football players must block out the cheering crowd to stay focused on the game. What other jobs or careers need one to shift their focus and block out distractions?
- What or who distracts you when you're trying to listen in class or stay focused?

STORY TIME

Hand out the Coloring Sheets and crayons or markers to younger students while the facilitator reads the story, if desired.

Distracted Dotty

> Dotty always seemed to get distracted. During science class, her best friend kept passing her notes. Dotty didn't want to be rude, but she also didn't want to miss the cool experiment they were doing. She wasn't sure what to do!
>
> Later, in reading time, a classmate kept talking. Dotty tried hard to focus on her book, but she kept

thinking about what her classmate was saying. She got so distracted she had to read the same paragraph three times!

When Dotty got home that afternoon and started on her homework, her little brother turned on the TV. That was the last straw! Dotty went to her room, closed the door, and made a big "Do Not Disturb" sign. Hanging it up gave her an idea.

The next morning, her brother kept asking her to play while she was getting ready for school. "We can play after school," Dotty told him. He giggled and ran off. Before science, she told her friend, "Let's talk during recess instead of passing notes." During reading, she said, "I feel distracted when you talk. Could you please be quiet?" Her classmate agreed.

That afternoon, Dotty proudly hung her "Do Not Disturb" sign on her door and finished her homework in record time. She felt happy and proud—she had found a way to stay focused!

DISCUSSION QUESTIONS

- What distracted Dotty when she was working?
- Make a connection to Dotty. What distracts you?
- What did Dotty say to her classmates when they were distracting her?
- How was Dotty proactive? How did she prevent the problem?
- What could Dotty say to herself to help her stay focused?

SKILL PRACTICE

Round 1: Follow the Leader

Place a plastic cup in the center of the table. Have students stand and make a circle around the table/cup. The leader (you) will say "clap," and the student will clap their hands. When you say "tap," they tap the table with both hands. When you say "grab," they grab the cup, and the person that grabs the cup first wins.

You will say "clap" and "tap" several times before saying "grab." For example, "clap, tap, tap, clap, tap, clap, clap, tap, clap, tap, tap, clap, tap, grab."

Optional rules: If students grab before you say "grab," they can keep going or sit down and watch.

After the game, debrief with the students. How did they stay focused during the game? What was the connection between the game and focus? (Why do they think we played this game during our focus lesson?)

Round 2: Add Distractions

Tell students they are going to play one more game, but this time with distractions.

Ask students to brainstorm strategies for managing distractions (including words they can say to themselves)—write answers on the board.

One student becomes the **Leader** and one the **Distractor**. The distractor tries to throw off the group (e.g., sounds, talking, funny faces) while they play.

Round 3: Rotate Turns

After each round, give students the chance to switch roles and experience being either the leader or the distractor. Once the game is finished, have a debriefing session where you ask students how they managed to stay focused despite the distractions. Discuss whether it was hard to stay focused as the leader and encourage them to think about how they can apply the distraction strategies in real life at school or home.

ADDITIONAL ACTIVITIES

ELEMENTARY

WINDCHIME LISTENING

You can find a windchime on Amazon but ask your school staff (like the music teacher), as they may have one as well. If you still don't have access to a windchime, you can also watch the *Cosmic Kids Yoga Super Listening* video (6 minutes): https://cosmickids.com/video/superpower-listening/.

Explain to students that their goal is to see how long they can hear the wind chime. It will start strong and gently fade away, but their goal is to see how long they can hear it. Ask students to look down and, if possible, close their eyes. Cue them to "look up" when they can no longer hear any sound from the wind chime. Ring the wind chime and wait until the last student has looked up.

Notice how we all heard the wind chime differently. When we are mindful, we notice the sounds around us, but sometimes we have to filter out the sounds around us to focus on one specific sound. In this case, it was the wind chime. When you are in class, what sounds do you have to filter out to focus on the teacher?

What else may distract us and prevent us from doing our best job listening?

Brainstorm and share. Answers may include others talking, the TV, our thoughts, sounds outside, music, etc.

ELEMENTARY MIDDLE/HIGH

MINDFUL LISTENING

Ask students to put their heads on their desk/on the table and, if they are comfortable, to close their eyes. If space allows you can also have students lie on the floor and spread out. See if they can notice a sound that is far away, even outside the room. Then see if they can notice a sound that is closer, in the room near them. Now see if they can notice a sound that is very close, perhaps the sound of their own breath. Invite them to open their eyes and share what they noticed.

ELEMENTARY MIDDLE/HIGH

BILATERAL SIMON SAYS

This game uses bilateral movement, where both sides of the body work together in a coordinated way. Bilateral activities strengthen the connection between the left and right hemispheres of the brain, which can improve focus, coordination, and cognitive flexibility.

Give each student two cups—one for each hand. Spread out colored pom poms on the table in front of them, making sure there are matching pairs (e.g., 2 yellows, 2 blues). Place one of each color on the student's left side and the matching one on the right side.

This activity is a twist on the classic game Simon Says. Call out, "Simon Says (insert color)," and students should use both hands at the same time to cover the pom poms of that color with their cups. For example, if you say, "Simon Says blue," they must use both hands to cover the blue pom poms. If you call out just the color without saying "Simon Says," they should freeze and not move.

Continue playing for as many rounds as you'd like, mixing up the colors and phrasing to keep it fun and challenging.

MIDDLE/HIGH

INTERVIEW SKILLS

If you're doing this activity with the whole class, pair students up so one can act as the interviewer and the other as the interviewee. If you prefer a small-group format, pick one student to be interviewed while the others take turns asking questions. Cut and hand out the **Interview Cards** included at the end of this chapter and let each interview last 2–3 minutes. Once the time is up, ask partners to discuss which active listening skills they noticed one another using and offer any suggestions for improvement. Then, have them switch roles so everyone gets a turn to practice both interviewing and being interviewed.

CLOSING CONSIDERATIONS

Today we practiced the EF skill of focus. When we are focused, we are better and more thoughtful listeners. We can help our PFC stay focused by eliminating distractions beforehand or by saying helpful things to ourselves and others if they are distracting us. This self-talk can encourage us to stay on topic and on task. How can what we practiced today help you in class or at home? How can it help you reach your goal?

Scaling Fist to Five

Ask students to reflect on today's session. Using their hands, ask them to put up the number that represents how they are feeling

- **0 (fist):** I feel totally overwhelmed and confused. I need lots of help.
- **3:** I understand it, but I need some support and practice.
- **5:** I feel confident. I could teach someone else all about this and how to do it.

"WOULD YOU RATHER?" GAME

Playing the "Would You Rather?" the game is a fun and engaging activity for students to develop their critical thinking skills. Students will reflect on their experience, evaluate their options based on their preferences, and reflect on the opinions of others, which provides different perspectives and strengthens the group's sense of connection to one another.

Would You Rather?

Review cards before playing and remove any that may not be relevant or developmentally appropriate for your students. Copy and cut out the questions for small groups to discuss. You can also have students sit/stand or have each person stand in the center of the room and move toward one side or the other to show their vote for either option as the facilitator reads the questions aloud.

DO YOUR HOMEWORK IN YOUR BEDROOM OR THE KITCHEN?	PUT YOUR PHONE AWAY SO YOU CAN'T SEE IT OR PUT IT ON "DO NOT DISTURB?"
PUT UP A "DO NOT DISTURB" SIGN ON YOUR DOOR OR POLITELY ASK PEOPLE TO COME BACK LATER WHEN YOU'RE TRYING TO FOCUS?	TAKE SHORT BREAKS OFTEN TO STAY FOCUSED OR WORK STRAIGHT THROUGH UNTIL YOU'RE FINISHED AND THEN TAKE A LONG BREAK?
STUDY IN A QUIET ROOM WITH NO DISTRACTIONS OR IN A BUSY PLACE WHILE WEARING HEADPHONES?	TRY TO STAY FOCUSED BY SITTING AT A CLEAN, EMPTY DESK OR HAVE A SMALL FIDGET TOY TO KEEP YOUR HANDS BUSY?

"There are always distractions, if you let them."
TONY LA RUSSA

Interview Cards

What is one skill you have that would help be successful at this job?

Why should we hire you?

What is one of your greatest strengths?

What is one of your weaknesses?

Why do you want this job?

How do you handle stress?

CHAPTER 6

RECALL AND MEMORY

MIND MAP

ELEMENTARY

On the board, draw a Mind Map, and ask students to consider the meaning of *Memory*.

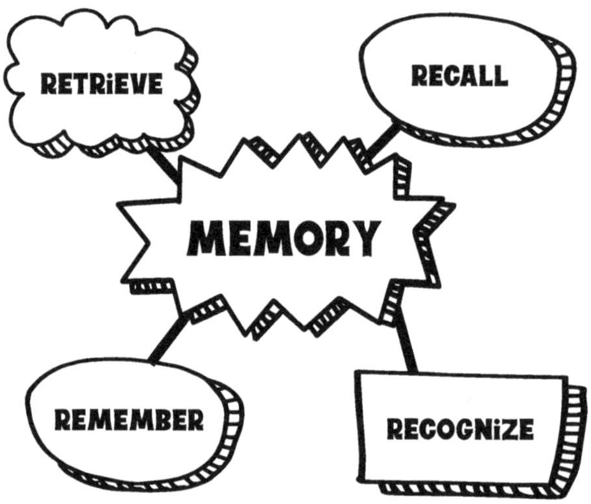

MIDDLE/HIGH

On the board, draw a Mind Map, and ask students to consider the meaning of *Hippocampus*.

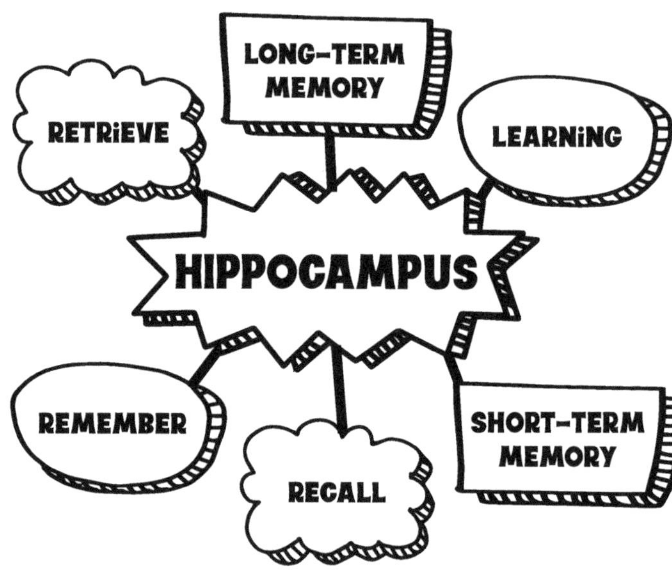

ASCA® STANDARDS

- **M 5.** Belief in using abilities to their fullest to achieve high-quality results and outcomes
- **B-LS 8.** Engagement in challenging coursework
- **B-SS 6.** Effective collaboration and cooperation skills

DIRECTIONS

- Begin the group by asking members to share a **Peak** and **Pit** from their week.

Share a positive or high moment from the week. Something that made you smile or feel good.

Share a low from the week. How did you get through it?

Alternatively, students can use an emotion scale to rate their feelings on a scale of 1 (not feeling great) to 10 (feeling their best).

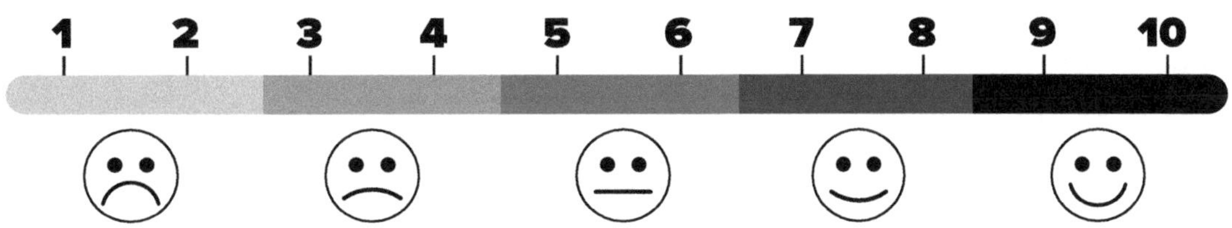

- Ask students to use the scale below to see how they're doing in reaching their goals. Our scale goes from 1 to 10: 1 means "I haven't started, or it's been really hard" and 10 means "I reached my goal!"

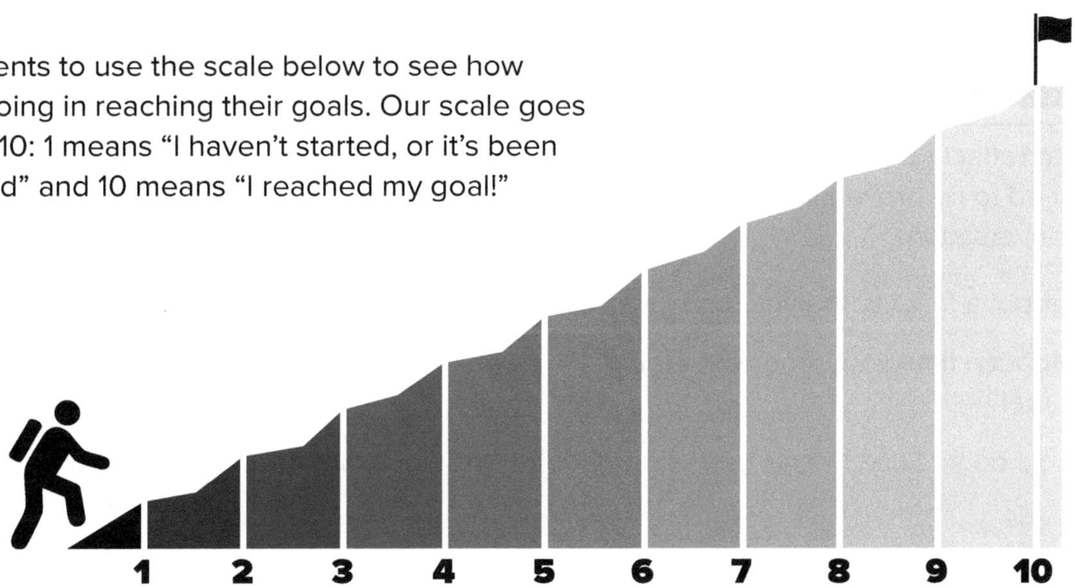

- Ask students to think about where they are on this scale and how they can move up? For example, if they're at a 4, what could they do to move up to a 5? Maybe they could try a new idea, ask a friend or adult for help, or change their plan. If they're at a 10, ask them to consider whether the goal was too easy. Could they try a bigger challenge next time?
- Review the Group Expectations.

- Read the Lesson Introduction and ask the Circle Time Questions before reading the Story and asking the Discussion Questions. Students can share individually or turn and talk to share their answers in pairs.
- Complete one of the Process Activities. If time allows, complete the Would You Rather cards (in a group or pairs) and Additional Activities.
- Be sure to complete the Closing Considerations with each lesson.

LESSON INTRODUCTION

Today, we're going to focus on strengthening our hippocampus, which is the part of our brain that helps us store and recall memories. Think of it as the brain's "save button" for important information. Memory is a key executive functioning (EF) skill because it allows us to remember what we need to do, recall facts for tests, and gather all our materials before we start an activity. It also helps us learn new things by transferring information from short-term memory (what you just heard) into long-term memory (what you remember for a long time).

Have you ever forgotten to bring your homework to school or missed an event because you didn't remember to go? How did you feel when that happened? Was there something distracting you, or did you simply forget to check your schedule?

Today, we'll play a few games that are designed to strengthen our hippocampus and improve our memory skills. By practicing these strategies, we can train our brains to remember important details, keep track of our tasks, and stay prepared for whatever comes our way!

CIRCLE TIME QUESTIONS

Ask students to reflect upon and share their answers to the following questions with the group. Larger groups may need to be broken into smaller groups to give students ample time to share their answers and deepen the conversation.

- Tell us about a favorite memory you have, a memory that makes you smile.
- Tell us about a time you forgot something you needed to do or somewhere you needed to be? How did you feel?
- What tools do you use to help you remember things? For example, sticky notes or alerts in your phone.

STORY TIME

Hand out the Coloring Sheets and crayons or markers to younger students while the facilitator reads the story, if desired.

Ellie Remembers!

Ellie was a most thoughtful friend. She always asked her friends how they were feeling, made sure no one was left out, and shared her snacks with everyone. But sometimes Ellie had trouble remembering important things, and it made her feel bad inside.

She forgot her friend's birthday, left a sweater at a friend's house, and even missed returning a phone call. Ellie would feel angry at herself when she forgot her homework or left an important paper at home. She didn't like the feeling of forgetting, and it made her frustrated.

One day, Ellie decided she needed help, so she asked someone she knew could help—her school counselor, Mrs. Shepherd. She told Mrs. Shepherd about how upset she was and how badly she wanted to get better at remembering things. Mrs. Shepherd listened carefully, gave Ellie some comforting words, and helped her come up with a plan to get better at remembering.

They started by making small changes. Ellie stuck a bright sticky note on her bathroom mirror each morning to remind her of the important things she had to do that day. She created a backpack checklist that she could check off each morning before school to make sure she had everything she needed. She even started putting important dates like birthdays, tests, and activities on a colorful calendar where she could easily see them.

Most importantly, Ellie knew she couldn't do it all on her own, so she asked a buddy at school to help remind her of important things. Every time Ellie felt like she was forgetting something, her buddy would give her a helpful reminder.

With these new habits, Ellie slowly began to feel more in control. She learned that it was okay to ask for help when you needed it, and creating systems to stay organized helped her feel less stressed. Soon, Ellie was remembering things much better, and she felt proud of how far she'd come. Now, instead of feeling guilty for forgetting, Ellie was able to focus on being the kind friend she always wanted to be—happy, helpful, and organized.

DISCUSSION QUESTIONS

- How did Ellie feel when she forgot things? Have you ever felt that way?
- Tell us about something that's hard for you to remember.
- What strategies did Ellie use to help her remember?
- Which of those strategies would you be willing to try?
- Tell us about a time when you successfully remembered to do something.

SKILL PRACTICE

Game Option 1:

Print two copies of the **Memory Match: Executive Function Skills** cards, for a total of 20 cards. Cut out the cards and place each set face down on the table.

Explain the rules of the game: Students will take turns flipping over two cards for everyone to see. If the cards match, they get to keep the pair. If the cards don't match, they will flip them back over, and the game continues with the next player's turn. The game continues until all matches have been found.

Game Option 2:

Print a set of the **Memory Match: Executive Function Skills** cards and the **Memory Match: Executive Function Strategy** cards on two different colored papers. Cut out the cards and place each set face down on the table, with one set on the right and the other on the left.

Explain the rules of the game: Students will take turns flipping over one card from the Skill set and one from the Strategy set. They should lay the cards they choose face up so everyone can see them. If the EF Skill matches the Strategy, the player keeps the cards. If they do not match, flip the cards back over and return them to the same spot. (See the Answer Key below.)

As an added activity, when using the Memory Match Executive Functioning Skill cards, have each student share one thing they remember about that skill or a piece of advice they would give someone who is struggling with that skill. When using Memory Match Executive Functioning Strategy Cards, have each student share an example of a time they would use this strategy or how they think using that strategy would help them.

Memory Match Answer Key

The Executive Function Skills cards match these Executive Function Strategies cards.

EXECUTIVE FUNCTION SKILLS	EXECUTIVE FUNCTION STRATEGIES
Memory	Use visual reminders
Focus	Turn off TV and phones
Planning	Break into small steps
Organization	Use a checklist
Prioritizing	Schedule tasks on calendar
Mindset	Say a helpful affirmation
Regulation	Take short breaks
Managing Frustration	Take deep breaths
Self-Monitoring	Track progress in a journal
Goal-Setting	Write your goal and keep it visible

ADDITIONAL ACTIVITIES

ELEMENTARY MIDDLE/HIGH

RETRIEVE IT/BRAIN DUMP

Provide each student with paper or writing materials—or record their responses on the board. Invite them to recall everything they've learned so far in group and write it down in any format they prefer, such as bullet points, sketches, or short sentences. There's no right or wrong way to do a brain dump; the goal is simply to capture as much information as possible from memory.

ELEMENTARY

SHOPPING LIST GAME

Begin by saying, "I went to the store and bought an....." The first item starts with the letter A. For example, "I went to the store and bought an avocado." Ask the next person to repeat your entire phrase, including the item you mentioned, and then add their own item that starts with the letter B. For example, they should say, "I went to the store and bought an avocado and a banana."

The next person will then repeat all previous items while adding one that begins with the letter C. For example, they might say, "I went to the store and bought an avocado, a banana, and a cat."

Continue around the group, with each person repeating all the items mentioned so far and then adding a new item that starts with the next letter of the alphabet (D, E, F, and so on).

To make it more fun, encourage everyone to choose unusual or silly items, like a smelly sock or a wacky hat, to spark laughter and creativity.

MIDDLE/HIGH

MNEMONIC DEVICE

Explain to students what a mnemonic device is. A mnemonic device is a tool that helps you remember information using associations, rhymes, or stories.

There are many types of mnemonic devices:

- **Acrostics:** Use the first letter of each word to create a phrase that helps you remember the words you want to recall.
- **Rhymes:** Use words that rhyme to help you remember facts. For instance, "i" comes before "e," except after "c," or in words that sound like "ay," such as "neighbor" or "weigh."
- **Imagery:** Use pictures, colors, and images to aid your memory.
- **Alliteration:** Connect words that start with the same letter to help you remember.

Examples:

- **Acronyms:**
    - Please Excuse My Dear Aunt Sally (Order of Operations in Math)
      Stands for "Parentheses, Exponents, Multiplication, Division, Addition, Subtraction."
    - HOMES (Great Lakes in Geography)
      Stands for "Huron, Ontario, Michigan, Erie, Superior."
    - ROY-G-BIV (Colors of the Rainbow)
      Stands for "Red, Orange, Yellow, Green, Blue, Indigo, Violet."

- **Rhyme:**
    - "Plan, focus, get it done,
      Think things through and have some fun!
      Stay flexible, manage time,
      Keep emotions in a line.
      Start a task and see it through,
      Remember what you need to do!
      Stay in control, don't miss a cue—
      Executive skills will help you!"
- **Alliteration:**
    - Plan, Prioritize, and Persevere!
      Plan (thinking ahead and making a strategy), *Prioritize* (deciding what's most important), *Persevere* (sticking with a task even when it's hard)
- **Imagery:**
    - A growling dog helps you remember the amygdala because it controls fear and emotions, just like a dog warns of danger.

Ask students to choose something they need to remember for a test or an important assignment. Have them create a mnemonic device for it.

CLOSING CONSIDERATIONS

Today we focused on the important skill of memory. A part of your brain called the hippocampus—shaped a bit like a seahorse—helps you remember what you learn and stores special memories. The hippocampus plays a big role in moving information from short-term to long-term memory, so you can recall it later when you need it.

There are many strategies to improve your memory, such as using mnemonic devices (like acronyms or silly sentences), creating visual maps, or even making up short stories about what you're learning. Whichever method you choose, practice it regularly until it becomes a habit. If one strategy doesn't make sense to you, try changing it or pick another that fits your style better. The key is to find a memory trick that resonates with you and keep practicing!

How can what we practiced today help you in class or at home? How can it help you reach your goal?

Scaling Fist to Five

Ask students to reflect on today's session. Using their hands, ask them to put up the number that represents how they are feeling

- **0 (fist):** I feel totally overwhelmed and confused. I need lots of help.
- **3:** I understand it, but I need some support and practice.
- **5:** I feel confident. I could teach someone else all about this and how to do it.

"WOULD YOU RATHER?" GAME

Playing the "Would You Rather?" the game is a fun and engaging activity for students to develop their critical thinking skills. Students will reflect on their experience, evaluate their options based on their preferences, and reflect on the opinions of others, which provides different perspectives and strengthens the group's sense of connection to one another.

WOULD YOU RATHER?

Review cards before playing and remove any that may not be relevant or developmentally appropriate for your students. Copy and cut out the questions for small groups to discuss. You can also have students sit/stand or have each person stand in the center of the room and move toward one side or the other to show their vote for either option as the facilitator reads the questions aloud.

HAVE A VERBAL OR WRITTEN REMINDER?	PUT A STICKY NOTE REMINDER ON YOUR MIRROR OR THE REFRIGERATOR?
USE A RHYME OR ACROSTIC TO HELP YOU REMEMBER?	HAVE A FRIEND OR TEACHER REMIND YOU ABOUT YOUR ASSIGNMENTS?
REMEMBER EVERY SINGLE FACT YOU EVER READ OR HAVE A PERFECT MEMORY FOR FACES AND NAMES?	NEVER FORGET YOUR HOMEWORK, OR NEVER FORGET THE CHORES YOU NEED TO DO AT HOME?

"The true art of memory is the art of attention."

SAMUEL JOHNSON

MEMORY

MEMORY MATCH
Executive Function Skills

FOCUS

MEMORY MATCH
Executive Function Skills

ORGANIZATION

MEMORY MATCH
Executive Function Skills

PLANNING

MEMORY MATCH
Executive Function Skills

PRIORITIZING

MEMORY MATCH
Executive Function Skills

MINDSET

MEMORY MATCH
Executive Function Skills

REGULATION

MEMORY MATCH
Executive Function Skills

MANAGING FRUSTRATION

MEMORY MATCH
Executive Function Skills

SELF-MONITORING

MEMORY MATCH
Executive Function Skills

GOAL SETTING

MEMORY MATCH
Executive Function Skills

MEMORY MATCH
Executive Function Strategies

Use Visual Reminders

MEMORY MATCH
Executive Function Strategies

Turn Off TV and Phones

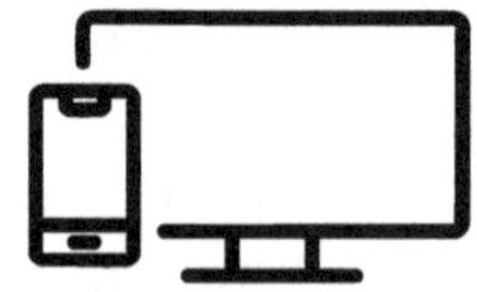

MEMORY MATCH
Executive Function Strategies

Break Into Small Steps

MEMORY MATCH
Executive Function Strategies

Use a Checklist

MEMORY MATCH
Executive Function Strategies

Schedule Tasks on Calendar

MEMORY MATCH
Executive Function Strategies

Say a Helpful Affirmation

MEMORY MATCH
Executive Function Strategies

Take Short Breaks

MEMORY MATCH
Executive Function Strategies

Take Deep Breaths

MEMORY MATCH
Executive Function Strategies

Track Progress in a Journal

MEMORY MATCH
Executive Function Strategies

Write Your Goal and Keep It Visible

CHAPTER 7

MiNDSET

MIND MAP

On the board, draw a Mind Map and ask students to consider the meaning of *Mindset*.

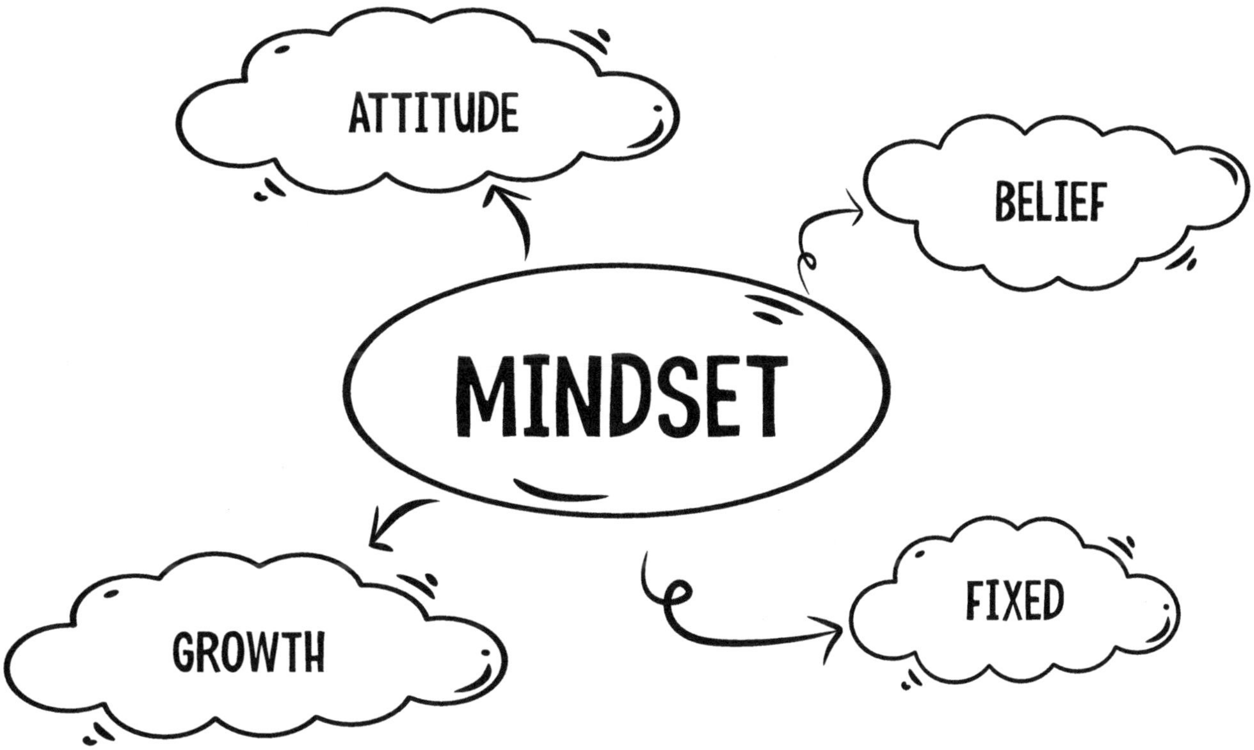

ASCA® STANDARDS

- **M 4.** Self-confidence in ability to succeed
- **M 5**. Belief in using abilities to their fullest to achieve high-quality results and outcomes
- **B-SMS 7**. Effective coping skills

DIRECTIONS

- Begin the group by asking members to share a **Peak** and **Pit** from their week.

Share a positive or high moment from the week. Something that made you smile or feel good.

Share a low from the week. How did you get through it?

Alternatively, students can use an emotion scale to rate their feelings on a scale of 1 (not feeling great) to 10 (feeling their best).

- Ask students to use the scale below to see how they're doing in reaching their goals. Our scale goes from 1 to 10: 1 means "I haven't started, or it's been really hard" and 10 means "I reached my goal!"

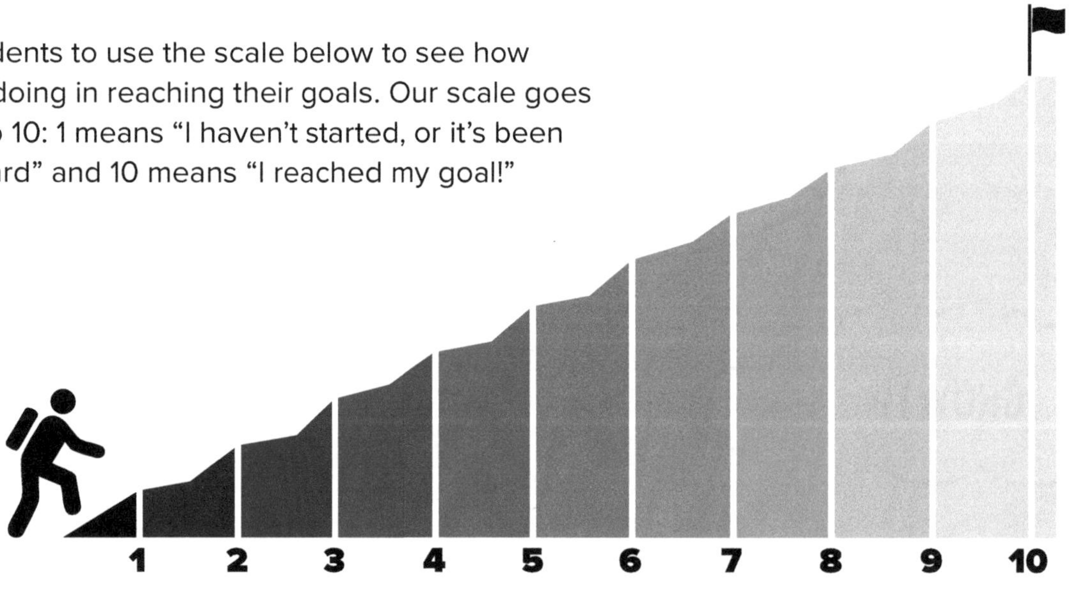

- Ask students to think about where they are on this scale and how they can move up? For example, if they're at a 4, what could they do to move up to a 5? Maybe they could try a new idea, ask a friend or adult for help, or change their plan. If they're at a 10, ask them to consider whether the goal was too easy. Could they try a bigger challenge next time?
- Review the Group Expectations.

- Read the Lesson Introduction and ask the Circle Time Questions before reading the Story and asking the Discussion Questions. Students can share individually or turn and talk to share their answers in pairs.
- Complete one of the Process Activities. If time allows, complete the Would You Rather cards (in a group or pairs) and Additional Activities.
- Be sure to complete the Closing Considerations with each lesson.

LESSON INTRODUCTION

Today, we're going to learn about having a helpful mindset, also known as a *growth mindset*. Our thoughts influence how we feel, and how we feel influences what we do. When we think helpful thoughts—like "I can learn this" or "I'll try again"—we feel more confident and strong, and we're more likely to reach our goals. That's the power of a *growth mindset*.

On the other hand, if we think unhelpful thoughts—like "I'm not good at this" or "I'll never figure it out"—we can feel frustrated or helpless. This *fixed mindset* might make us give up or not even try. The good news is, if we change our thoughts, we can change our feelings and actions too! Let's explore how we can practice a growth mindset.

CIRCLE TIME QUESTIONS

Ask students to reflect upon and share their answers to the following questions with the group. Larger groups may need to be broken into smaller groups to give students ample time to share their answers and deepen the conversation.

- Imagine you're taking a test, and you get to a really hard question. What are some things that your brain might say? What thoughts may you have?
- Can you think of a book character, celebrity, or person in your life that has dealt with failure but kept going?
- What do you think a growth mindset sounds like? Feels like? What does it look like?

STORY TIME

Hand out the Coloring Sheets and crayons or markers to younger students while the facilitator reads the story, if desired.

Humpty's Great Rise

> You know Humpty Dumpty, right? The egg who had a great fall? Everyone said he couldn't be put back together—but they were wrong! He was fixed up, good as new. But what happened after that fall? Well, that's where the real story begins.

After his tumble, Humpty was scared to climb. "What if I fall again?" he worried. So instead of daring adventures, he stuck to safe hobbies—like baking. And wow, could he bake! Cookies, cupcakes, birthday cakes—you name it. He even baked for the King's horses and men!

One day, he tried inventing a new treat: lemon-strawberry layered cookies. But the first batch was *too sweet*. The second? *Too sour*. The third? *Burnt to a crisp!*

"I give up!" he sighed to his friend, Puss in Boots.

"Don't quit yet," said Puss. "Ever hear how chocolate chip cookies were invented? Ruth Wakefield didn't *mean* to invent them—she just ran out of chocolate and tried something new. It didn't melt, and boom! A new cookie was born."

"Really?" Humpty blinked.

"Yep! Accidents, practice, and patience—that's how great things happen."

Humpty smiled. "I *can* do hard things."

He baked again and again—tweaking, testing, trying—until he got it just right. The perfect lemon-strawberry cookies!

That little success gave him a big idea. "If I can figure out cookies, maybe I can climb again."

So he walked to a mountain, heart pounding. "I can do this," he whispered. "I can be scared and brave." Step by step, he climbed. And when he reached the top, he grinned from ear to ear. The view was amazing—and so was the feeling of courage bubbling inside.

DISCUSSION QUESTIONS

- How do you think Humpty felt after his fall? Have you ever felt like that?
- Humpty wanted to start baking. What is something you want to try, but have been too scared to try?
- What helped Humpty achieve his goals?
- What advice do you think Humpty could give our group?
- What examples of fixed and growth mindsets did you hear in the story?

SKILL PRACTICE

Print and cut out the **Mindset Cards** included at the end of this chapter. Place the mindset cards face down in the center of the table.

Each student will take a turn picking a card and reading it aloud. If the card has a growth mindset statement, the student shares a situation or time when thinking that way would be helpful. If the card has a fixed mindset statement, the student either rips it up or uses the mini shredder while explaining how they could reframe it into a more helpful, growth-oriented thought.

If you are doing this activity with the whole class, students can first partner up and take turns sharing what's written on their cards. Partners will decide together if the statement shows a growth or fixed mindset. Another option is for you to read each card aloud to the entire class. If the statement shows a growth mindset, students give a thumbs-up. If it shows a fixed mindset, students give a thumbs-down.

Afterward, give each student two blank mindset cards or a piece of paper and writing materials. Ask them to write one example of a growth mindset statement and one example of a fixed mindset statement based on their own experiences. Collect all of the new statements.

Then, repeat the original activity by reading each new statement, deciding whether it represents a growth or fixed mindset, and practicing how to reframe the fixed statements into more helpful, growth-focused thoughts.

ADDITIONAL ACTIVITIES

ELEMENTARY MIDDLE/HIGH

WOW AND HOW?

Invite each student to think of a time they overcame a challenge and share it with the group by completing the sentence, "Wow, guess what I did? I _____." Once the student finishes, have the entire class respond in unison with "How?" to encourage them to explain the steps or strategies they used to succeed. This activity helps students reflect on their own problem-solving skills while also celebrating each other's achievements.

ELEMENTARY

BUBBLE THOUGHTS

Today we talked about our mindsets. Our thoughts can help us have a growth mindset, which takes us closer to our goals, or they can create a fixed mindset, where we get stuck in the mud. Our thoughts are like bubbles: they just "pop" into our heads. Sometimes, just like when we blow bubbles, we have lots of them. Maybe our brain has many thought bubbles popping up all at once. So, we need to "pop" some bubbles so we can stay focused and make room for other thoughts.

As a group, let's come up with examples of distracting thoughts—things that might pop into our minds and make it hard to concentrate. (For example: "What's for lunch?", "Did I do okay on that test?", or "I wonder what my dog is doing right now.")

As each person shares a distracting thought, we'll imagine it as a bubble and then pop it to let it go. This helps us clear space in our brain to focus on what's important right now. Other examples of thoughts we may want to "pop" are unhelpful thoughts.

As you blow bubbles, read the examples of different types of thoughts. If it's a helpful thought or shows a growth mindset, tell students to let the bubble stay or float away. If it's an unhelpful thought or shows a fixed mindset, have students pop the bubble to let it go.

(Read as many examples as you'd like or as time allows.)

- This homework is too hard.
- I will never be as good as them.
- I don't understand this, YET!
- Waking up for school is hard, but at least I see my friends.
- They cheated.
- Everyone has to like me.
- Some people might not like that, but that's okay.
- I don't want to be their friend.
- That was a good game, even if I didn't win.
- This isn't a big deal.
- Change is scary, but I can handle it.
- What if I fail?
- This is boring.

MIDDLE/HIGH

FAMOUS OVERCOMERS

Have students choose an inventor, writer, athlete, actor, celebrity, or someone they know personally who has overcome challenges. Ask them to research this individual's story and identify moments when they demonstrated a growth mindset. Students should then create a presentation—such as a drawing, poster, video, or PowerPoint—that includes quotes, examples, and specific details showing how their chosen person persevered in difficult situations.

CLOSING CONSIDERATIONS

Today we talked about how our mindset can help us persevere when we face a challenge. Hard work, practice, feedback, and even mistakes help us grow and get better. Challenges give us chances to improve and having a growth mindset can help us through the struggle.

How can what we practiced today help you in class or at home? How can it help you reach your goal?

Scaling Fist to Five

Ask students to reflect on today's session. Using their hands, ask them to put up the number that represents how they are feeling

- **0 (fist):** I feel totally overwhelmed and confused. I need lots of help.
- **3:** I understand it, but I need some support and practice.
- **5:** I feel confident. I could teach someone else all about this and how to do it.

"WOULD YOU RATHER?" GAME

Playing the "Would You Rather?" the game is a fun and engaging activity for students to develop their critical thinking skills. Students will reflect on their experience, evaluate their options based on their preferences, and reflect on the opinions of others, which provides different perspectives and strengthens the group's sense of connection to one another.

WOULD YOU RATHER?

Review cards before playing and remove any that may not be relevant or developmentally appropriate for your students. Copy and cut out the questions for small groups to discuss. You can also have students sit/stand or have each person stand in the center of the room and move toward one side or the other to show their vote for either option as the facilitator reads the questions aloud.

ASK FOR HELP WHEN YOU'RE STUCK ON A MATH PROBLEM, OR TRY TO FIGURE IT OUT FIRST, EVEN IF IT TAKES LONGER?	LISTEN TO AN APP FILLED WITH ENCOURAGING AFFIRMATIONS, OR READ A BOOK PACKED WITH POSITIVE MINDSET EXAMPLES?
TELL YOURSELF "I DON'T HAVE TO BE PERFECT" OR REMIND YOURSELF "I CAN GET BETTER WITH PRACTICE" WHENEVER SOMETHING IS TOUGH?	KEEP PRACTICING A SKILL THAT'S DIFFICULT FOR YOU, OR FOCUS ON SOMETHING YOU'RE ALREADY GOOD AT SO YOU FEEL MORE COMFORTABLE?
TRY SOMETHING TOTALLY NEW (EVEN IF IT'S HARD) TO LEARN FRESH SKILLS, OR KEEP IMPROVING A SKILL YOU ALREADY KNOW WELL?	CELEBRATE SMALL IMPROVEMENTS YOU NOTICE EACH DAY, OR WAIT UNTIL YOU COMPLETELY MASTER A SKILL BEFORE CELEBRATING?

"Our greatest glory is not in never falling, but in rising every time we fall"

NELSON MANDELA

Mindset Cards

Show each card to students or a classmate and ask them to determine whether the statement is a **Fixed Mindset** or **Growth Mindset**.

I can learn from my mistakes.

FIXED MINDSET — GROWTH MINDSET

I can't do this YET.

FIXED MINDSET — GROWTH MINDSET

I can handle hard things.

FIXED MINDSET — GROWTH MINDSET

This is too hard.

FIXED MINDSET — GROWTH MINDSET

Mistakes mean I'm not good enough.

FIXED MINDSET — GROWTH MINDSET

I'll never understand.

FIXED MINDSET — GROWTH MINDSET

Mindset Cards

Show each card to students or a classmate and ask them to determine whether the statement is a **Fixed Mindset** or **Growth Mindset**.

I don't like to be challenged.

FIXED MINDSET | GROWTH MINDSET

I'm going to try a different strategy.

FIXED MINDSET | GROWTH MINDSET

If I fail, it means I'm a failure.

FIXED MINDSET | GROWTH MINDSET

Practice makes progress.

FIXED MINDSET | GROWTH MINDSET

I'm just not good at this.

FIXED MINDSET | GROWTH MINDSET

What can I learn from this feedback?

FIXED MINDSET | GROWTH MINDSET

Mindset Cards

Show each card to students or a classmate and ask them to determine whether the statement is a **Fixed Mindset** or **Growth Mindset**.

I am constantly growing my abilities.

FIXED MINDSET | GROWTH MINDSET

I can improve if I keep working at it.

FIXED MINDSET | GROWTH MINDSET

Other people are just naturally better than me.

FIXED MINDSET | GROWTH MINDSET

I can take small steps and get closer to my goal!

FIXED MINDSET | GROWTH MINDSET

FIXED MINDSET | GROWTH MINDSET

FIXED MINDSET | GROWTH MINDSET

CHAPTER 8

Self-Regulation

MIND MAP

On the board, draw a mind map and ask students to consider the meaning of *Self-Regulation*.

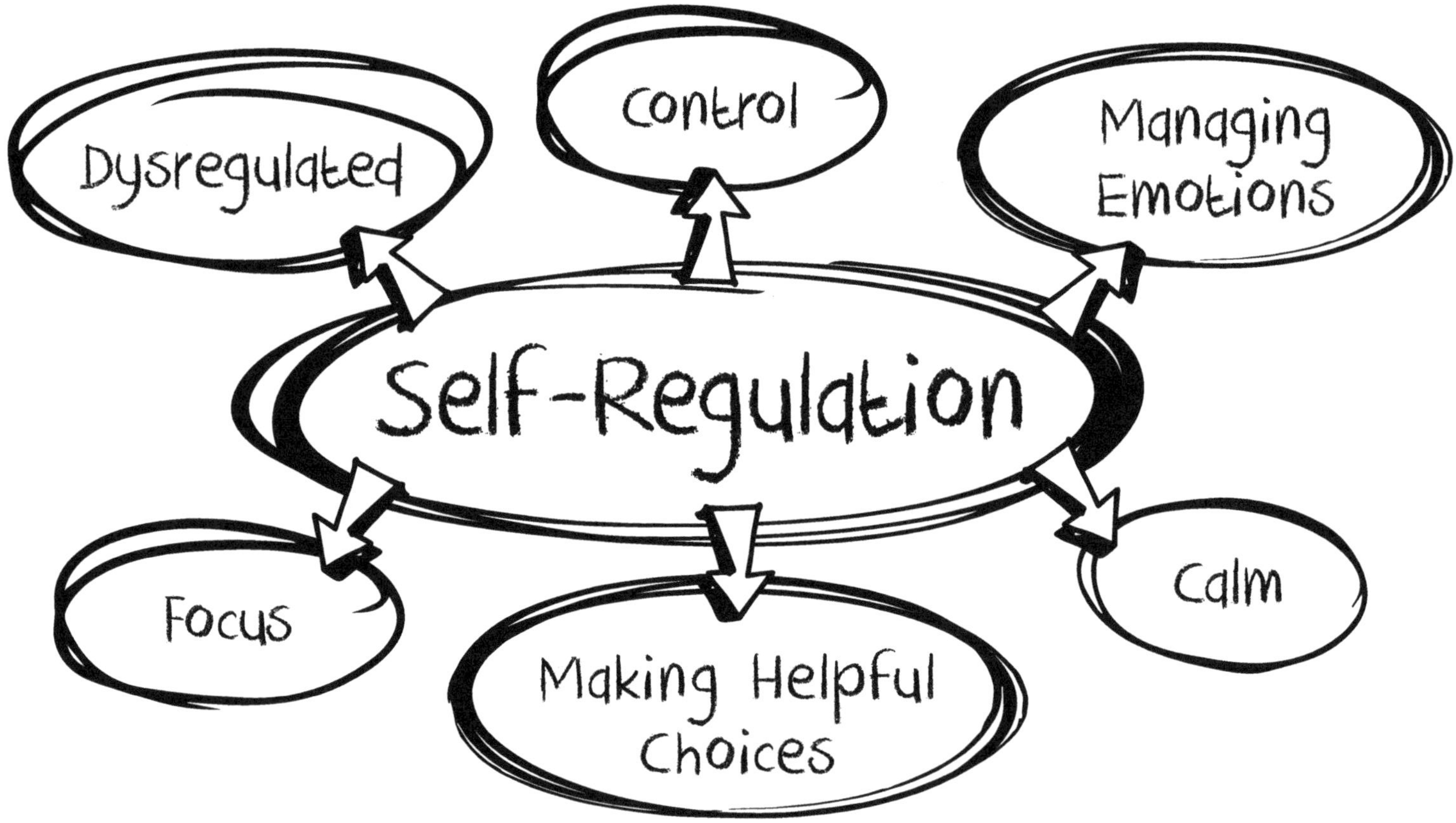

ASCA® STANDARDS

- **B-SMS 2.** Self-discipline and self-control
- **B-SS 6.** Effective collaboration and cooperation skills
- **B-SS 2.** Positive, respectful and supportive relationships with students who are similar to and different from them

DIRECTIONS

- Begin the group by asking members to share a **Peak** and **Pit** from their week.

Share a positive or high moment from the week. Something that made you smile or feel good.

Share a low from the week. How did you get through it?

Alternatively, students can use an emotion scale to rate their feelings on a scale of 1 (not feeling great) to 10 (feeling their best).

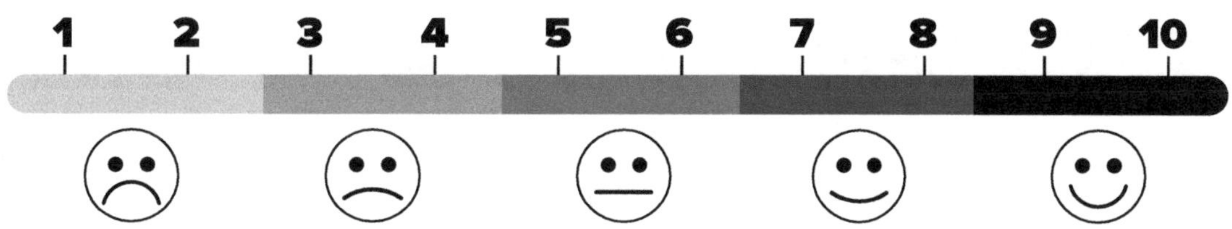

- Ask students to use the scale below to see how they're doing in reaching their goals. Our scale goes from 1 to 10: 1 means "I haven't started, or it's been really hard" and 10 means "I reached my goal!"

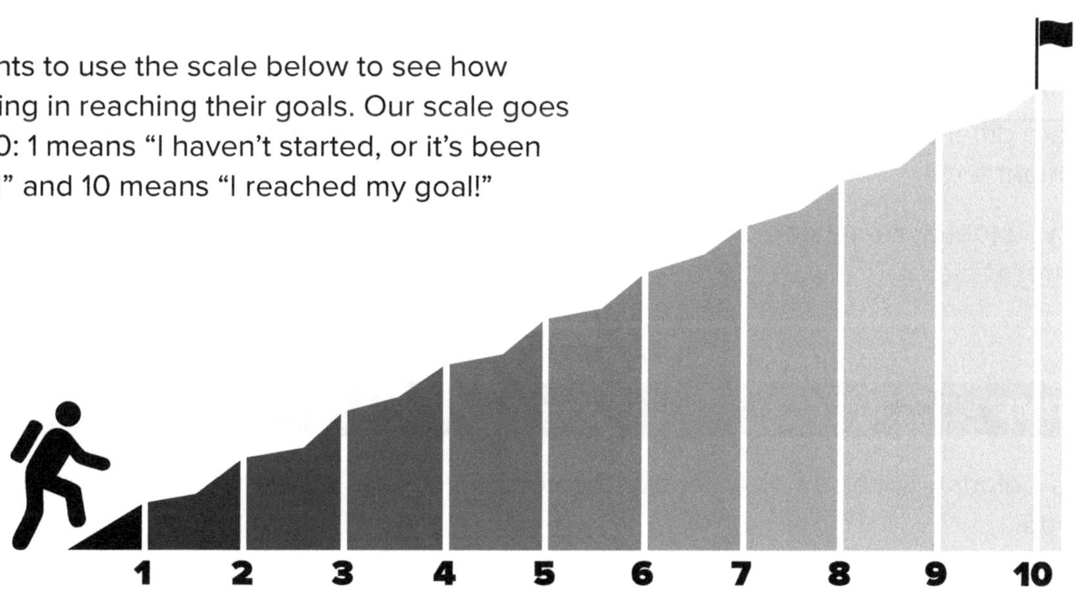

- Ask students to think about where they are on this scale and how they can move up? For example, if they're at a 4, what could they do to move up to a 5? Maybe they could try a new idea, ask a friend or adult for help, or change their plan. If they're at a 10, ask them to consider whether the goal was too easy. Could they try a bigger challenge next time?
- Review the Group Expectations.

- Read the Lesson Introduction and ask the Circle Time Questions before reading the Story and asking the Discussion Questions. Students can share individually or turn and talk to share their answers in pairs.
- Complete one of the Process Activities. If time allows, complete the Would You Rather cards (in a group or pairs) and Additional Activities.
- Be sure to complete the Closing Considerations with each lesson.

LESSON INTRODUCTION

Today we are going to talk about self-regulation. When we are regulated we are calm, alert, and ready to learn. Our PFC is in control and we make helpful choices we feel proud of. However, sometimes things happen that cause our amygdala to "bark." When our amygdala is in control, we become dysregulated. Our hearts beat faster, our thoughts go wild, and our muscles might tense up. When this happens we can make mistakes we regret. Dysregulation is not a feeling, it's what happens to our bodies. Today we are going to talk about what happens in our bodies when we get dysregulated and practice skills that can help us stay in control.

CIRCLE TIME QUESTIONS

Ask students to reflect and share their answers to the following questions with the group. Larger groups may need to be broken into smaller groups to give students ample time to share their answers and deepen the conversation.

- Tell us about a rule (at school or home) that is hard to follow, but you do it anyway.
- What is something you do to calm down when you feel upset?
- What are different emotions we may feel that cause us to feel out of control or dysregulated? (anger, excitement, etc.)
- When you feel dysregulated and out of control, what do you do? What is your typical response (fight, flight, freeze, fawn)?

STORY TIME

Hand out the Coloring Sheets and crayons or markers to younger students while the facilitator reads the story, if desired.

Josie's Big Energy

> Josie loved school—maybe a little too much. During story time, whenever her teacher read an exciting part of the book, Josie would blurt out what she noticed and sometimes even give away the ending. At lunch, she was so eager to share every detail of her week that she talked with her mouth full, sending bits of food flying. During recess, her excitement led her to run too fast or push too hard, sometimes knocking people down.

One day, the class held a meeting to share how they were feeling. Josie interrupted every time someone spoke, eager to tell a story of her own. When it was Ben's turn, he began to talk about feeling sad, but Josie cut him off. "Stop!" Ben said. "I'm sorry, Josie, but please don't interrupt. We feel frustrated when you won't let us have a turn." The whole class nodded in agreement.

"I didn't realize how much it bothered everyone," Josie said quietly.
"We love playing with you," Laura added, "but sometimes you push too hard, run too fast, and don't take turns."

Josie felt embarrassed; she hadn't meant to overwhelm her friends.

Her teacher, Mrs. Norton, spoke up. "Class, I'm proud of you for sharing your feelings. It's not always easy to have so much energy, and when we can't control it, we sometimes make unhelpful choices. Let me show you a strategy that helps me—it's called a wall push."

Mrs. Norton walked to the wall and stood so her feet were flat on the floor and her arms could reach out in front of her. Then she pushed against the wall as hard as she could. The class joined in. "Wall pushes help when we have lots of energy to get out," she explained.

Later that day, Josie felt that rush of energy in her toes right before recess. She wanted to dash outside at full speed, but she remembered what Mrs. Norton had taught her. Instead, Josie went over to the wall and did a wall push. Mrs. Norton saw her and smiled. "I'm so proud of you, Josie," she said. Josie beamed with pride as she calmly walked out to recess, feeling in control of her big energy.

DISCUSSION QUESTIONS

- Was Josie regulated (calm, alert, and ready to learn) or dysregulated (full of energy, unfocused, and not ready to learn) at the start of the story? How do you know?
- Which unhelpful choices did Josie make because she was so excited or energetic?
- How do you think her body felt with all that energy? Describe the sensations she might have experienced.
- Have you ever felt like Josie—so full of energy that it was hard to stay in control?
- When might you use a wall push in your own life to help manage strong energy or feelings?

SKILL PRACTICE

Practice a Wall Push together.

- Stand facing a wall with your feet shoulder-width apart.
- Place your palms flat against the wall at shoulder height.
- Push firmly into the wall, engaging your arms and core, while maintaining a straight back.
- Focus on the sensation of your hands pressing against the wall and your feet connecting to the floor.
- Breathe deeply and steadily while pushing.

Distribute the **Say It and Soothe It Activity Sheet** and provide each student with a pencil or pen. Read each emotion listed on the sheet aloud, and explain any that students may not understand.

Next, invite students to think of a time when they felt that emotion. Then, have them choose a coping skill they believe would help them stay regulated or calm and make positive choices in that situation.

In the square below each emoji, students should write the letter that matches the coping skill they think would be most helpful.

Finally, ask students to create their own examples at the bottom of the page by completing the sentence "When I feel ____, I can ____." Offer an example like, "When I feel extra energetic, I can exercise or push on a wall." Encourage them to share their responses with the group or a partner, highlighting how recognizing emotions and using coping strategies can help them manage strong feelings.

ADDITIONAL ACTIVITIES

ELEMENTARY **MIDDLE/HIGH**

FIND THE PAUSE

Cue students to close their eyes or turn their gaze downward and away from others. Ask students to notice their breath. Ask them to notice how their chest and belly rise, hover, and fall with each breath. Now ask them to "find the pause"—the moment between their inhale and their exhale. Have them go through several rounds of breathing, each time finding the pause. Invite students to open their eyes or look up. Take time to allow students to share with the group or with partners how they felt during the activity and what they noticed.

ELEMENTARY

RED LIGHT/ GREEN LIGHT

Have all the players line up on one side of the room or field, facing you. Explain that when you say, "Green Light," they should move forward, but when you say, "Red Light," they must freeze immediately. If anyone is caught moving after you say, "Red Light," they should return to the starting line (or take a step back, depending on your rules). The first person to reach you wins. Encourage everyone to move safely, without running into each other or pushing. After one round is complete, let a new student take your place as the caller, and play again.

MIDDLE/HIGH

TURN UP THE VOLUME

Explain to students that they will move around the room in any safe way they choose—such as walking, dancing, or skipping. Let them know that the music's volume will guide their pace: when the volume goes up, they should speed up, and when it goes down, they should slow down. Remind them to stay aware of their surroundings and respect everyone's space so that everyone can enjoy the activity safely.

CLOSING CONSIDERATIONS

We make choices every day—from what we eat to what we wear—and we're responsible for the results of those choices. Remember, "You're free to choose, but you're not free from the consequences of your choice." That's why it's important to pause and regulate our emotions before deciding what to do next. We can do this by taking a short break, doing a wall push, breathing deeply, or naming our feelings. Understanding how we feel helps us manage those emotions. This isn't just for when we're upset. Sometimes, we're full of energy and need a moment to calm our brains and bodies so we're alert, focused, and ready to learn.

How can what we practiced today help you in class or at home? How can it help you reach your goal?

Scaling Fist to Five

Ask students to reflect on today's session. Using their hands, ask them to put up the number that represents how they are feeling

- **0 (fist):** I feel totally overwhelmed and confused. I need lots of help.
- **3:** I understand it, but I need some support and practice.
- **5:** I feel confident. I could teach someone else all about this and how to do it.

"WOULD YOU RATHER?" GAME

Playing the "Would You Rather?" the game is a fun and engaging activity for students to develop their critical thinking skills. Students will reflect on their experience, evaluate their options based on their preferences, and reflect on the opinions of others, which provides different perspectives and strengthens the group's sense of connection to one another.

Would You Rather?

Review cards before playing and remove any that may not be relevant or developmentally appropriate for your students. Copy and cut out the questions for small groups to discuss. You can also have students sit/stand or have each person stand in the center of the room and move toward one side or the other to show their vote for either option as the facilitator reads the questions aloud.

RELEASE EXTRA ENERGY BY RUNNING OR BY SWIMMING?	DO A WALL PUSH OR TAKE A WATER BREAK WHEN YOU'RE FEELING RESTLESS?
HAVE INDOOR RECESS OR OUTDOOR RECESS TO HELP YOU RECHARGE?	SCHEDULE A BREAK AT THE SAME TIME EVERY DAY OR TAKE A BREAK ONLY WHEN YOU FEEL YOU NEED IT?
DO TEN JUMPING JACKS OR STRETCH FOR TWO MINUTES WHEN YOU START FEELING FIDGETY?	TAKE A MINUTE TO PRACTICE DEEP BREATHING OR SPEND A MINUTE SQUEEZING A STRESS BALL WHEN YOU START TO FEEL OVERWHELMED?

"If you learn
self-control you can
master anything."
UNKNOWN

Say It and Soothe It

In the square below each emoji, write the letter for the coping skill you feel would be most effective.

WORRIED/ANXIOUS

FRUSTRATED

SAD

DISAPPOINTED

CONFUSED

SURPRISED/SCARED

OVERWHELMED

EMBARRASSED

LONELY

JEALOUS

COPING SKILLS

A. Take Deep Breaths: Find a quiet moment and focus on your breath. Inhale slowly through your nose, hold for a few seconds, and exhale slowly through your mouth. Repeat this several times.

B. Find a Quiet Space: If you're feeling overwhelmed, try to find a calm and quiet spot for a few minutes. This could be at your desk, in a Calm Corner, or even just stepping out into the hallway briefly (if allowed and safe).

C. Do a Quick Body Scan: Pay attention to how your body is feeling. Are your shoulders tense? Is your stomach in knots? Simply noticing these physical sensations can help you become more aware of your emotions and start to release tension.

D. Talk to a Trusted Adult: If you're comfortable, reach out to a teacher, counselor, school psychologist, or another adult you trust. Talking about how you're feeling can be really helpful.

E. Engage Your Senses: Focus on something specific you can see, hear, smell, touch, or taste. This can help ground you in the present moment and distract you from overwhelming feelings. For example, notice the texture of your desk, the sound of the birds outside, or the scent of hand sanitizer.

F. Write It Down: If you have a notebook or even a scrap of paper, jot down how you're feeling. You don't have to write in complete sentences, just getting your feelings out on paper can be a release.

G. Do a Gentle Stretch: If you're feeling tense, try some simple stretches like rolling your shoulders, stretching your arms, or gently moving your neck. This can help release physical tension that often comes with strong emotions.

H. Use a Fidget Tool (if allowed): If you have a small, quiet fidget toy (like a stress ball or a smooth stone), using it can help you focus your energy and reduce feelings of anxiety or restlessness. Make sure it's not distracting to others.

I. Visualize a Calm Place: Close your eyes for a moment and imagine a place where you feel safe and peaceful. Focus on the details of this place – what does it look like, sound like, smell like? This mental escape can be very soothing.

J. Take a Short Walk (if permitted): If you're allowed to, a brief walk around the classroom or down the hallway (with permission) can help you clear your head and release some energy.

"When I feel____________________ I can______________________________."

"When I feel____________________ I can______________________________."

"When I feel____________________ I can______________________________."

CHAPTER 9

MANAGING FRUSTRATION

MIND MAP

ELEMENTARY

On the board, draw a Mind Map, and ask students to consider the meaning of *Frustration*.

MIDDLE/HIGH

On the board, draw a Mind Map, and ask students to consider the meaning of *Amygdala*.

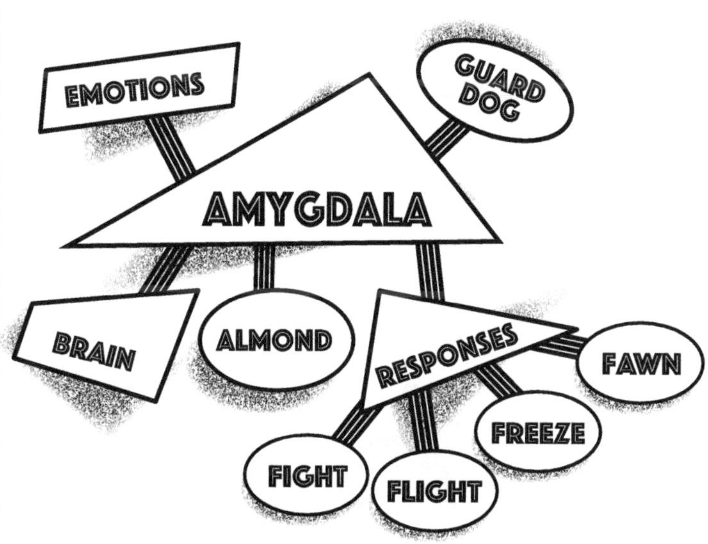

ASCA® STANDARDS

- **B-LS 4.** Self-motivation and self-direction for learning
- **B-SMS 7.** Effective coping skills

DIRECTIONS

- Begin the group by asking members to share a **Peak** and **Pit** from their week.

Share a positive or high moment from the week. Something that made you smile or feel good.

Share a low from the week. How did you get through it?

Alternatively, students can use an emotion scale to rate their feelings on a scale of 1 (not feeling great) to 10 (feeling their best).

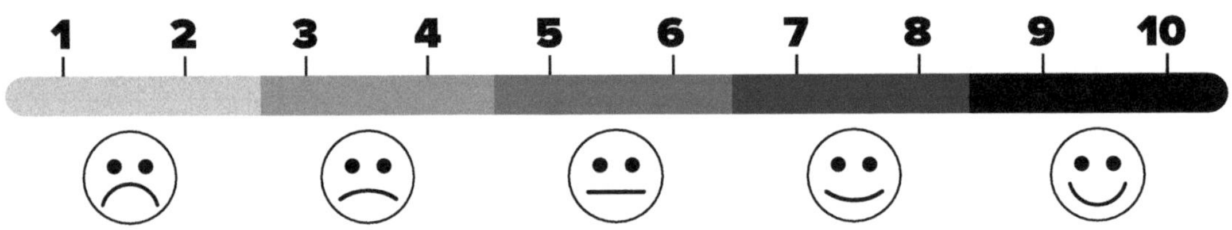

- Ask students to use the scale below to see how they're doing in reaching their goals. Our scale goes from 1 to 10: 1 means "I haven't started, or it's been really hard" and 10 means "I reached my goal!"

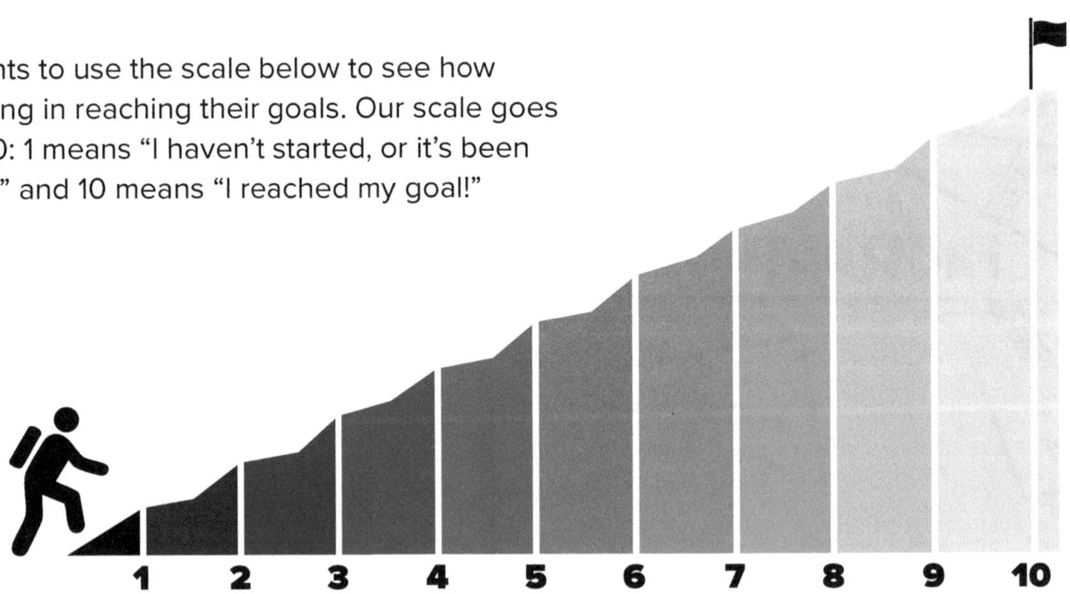

- Ask students to think about where they are on this scale and how they can move up? For example, if they're at a 4, what could they do to move up to a 5? Maybe they could try a new idea, ask a friend or adult for help, or change their plan. If they're at a 10, ask them to consider whether the goal was too easy. Could they try a bigger challenge next time?
- Review the Group Expectations.

- Read the Lesson Introduction and ask the Circle Time Questions before reading the Story and asking the Discussion Questions. Students can share individually or turn and talk to share their answers in pairs.
- Complete one of the Process Activities. If time allows, complete the Would You Rather cards (in a group or pairs) and Additional Activities.
- Be sure to complete the Closing Considerations with each lesson.

LESSON INTRODUCTION

We all feel frustrated sometimes, and that's perfectly normal. Frustrating things can happen every day—maybe your schedule changes unexpectedly, or a friend says something hurtful. It can be especially tough when we have no control over the situation. It's okay to feel frustrated, but we're still in charge of how we respond. Today, we'll explore ways to cope with these challenging feelings.

CIRCLE TIME QUESTIONS

Ask students to reflect upon and share their answers to the following questions with the group. Larger groups may need to be broken into smaller groups to give students ample time to share their answers and deepen the conversation.

- Fill in the blanks to describe how you feel and how your body reacts: "When I feel ____, my body ____." For example, "When I feel angry, my body tightens up," or "When I feel scared, my legs feel like Jello."
- Think about a time when you felt really frustrated. What happened, and how did you respond?
- Identify situations that might be out of your control and cause frustration. How could you cope with them?

STORY TIME

Hand out the Coloring Sheets and crayons or markers to younger students while the facilitator reads the story, if desired.

Bindu's Big Growl

> Most of the time, Bindu was a carefree, happy puppy. She loved running after her ball, chasing butterflies, and playing tug-of-war with her friends. But sometimes things happened that made her angry. If a bigger dog snatched her favorite chew toy, Bindu would let out a low snarl. If the neighbor's cat teased her from behind the fence, she'd bark and growl in frustration, even though she couldn't do much about it.
>
> One morning, a sudden thunderstorm rolled in. Bindu had no control over the loud thunder or the flashing lightning, but it still upset her. She tried to ignore it, but her tail tucked between her legs and her ears flattened against her head. Then her friend, a playful puppy named Riley, accidentally bumped into her while racing around the house. That was one thing too many for Bindu. She let out a huge growl, surprising everyone—including herself.

Bindu felt embarrassed and overwhelmed. She didn't want to scare her friends, but she also didn't know how to handle all the things bothering her. Her owner, noticing how upset Bindu was, knelt down and showed her a new trick: slow, deep breathing. At first, Bindu tilted her head in confusion. Breathing was something she already did, right? But when she tried it on purpose—inhale slowly, exhale slowly—she felt a little calmer.

Soon, Bindu realized there were some things she could control, like her breathing or how she reacted when her toy got snatched. Other things, like thunderstorms or teasing cats, were out of her control. She practiced taking deep breaths whenever she felt her anger rising. Over time, she found it easier to stay calm and playful, even when storms rumbled overhead, or a cat teased her from the fence.

And the next time a friend accidentally bumped into her, Bindu took a long, deep breath before any growls could escape. She wagged her tail instead, feeling proud that she was learning to manage her big feelings, one breath at a time.

DISCUSSION QUESTIONS

- What made Bindu upset? Were these problems small, medium, or really big deals?
- Which things could Bindu control, and which things were outside of her control?
- What strategy helped Bindu calm down when she felt frustrated?
- Have you ever felt like Bindu? Share a time when you felt upset and how you handled it.
- If you were Bindu's friend, what advice would you give her to manage her anger before it becomes a big growl?

SKILL PRACTICE

Explain the purpose of the activity to students: "Scientists who study the brain have found that focusing on your breathing can help you calm down. Taking slow, deep breaths lowers your heart rate and gives you time to think before reacting. It also helps the part of your brain called the amygdala—which acts like an alarm for big emotions—become less reactive. By slowing down and breathing, we can feel calmer and make better choices when we're upset."

"Many studies show deep breathing and mindfulness can improve focus, reduce stress, and help us feel more in control of our emotions."

Teach students **Bird Breathing**. Stand up tall with a lot of space between each student. As they inhale, they extend their arms out to the side and then raise them overhead, like bird wings flapping. As they exhale, their arms lower back down to their sides.

Now practice **Cupcake Breathing**. Ask students to imagine your favorite kind of cupcake or cake. Maybe it's chocolate, vanilla, or strawberry. Imagine it is warm and straight from the oven, so it's nice and hot and decorated with a candle on top. As they inhale, they pretend they are smelling the cupcake, and, as they exhale, they pretend to blow out the candle.

Next is **Finger Breathing**. Have students pretend they are giving you an air high five. Using their pointer finger, they trace one finger at a time. As they trace up a finger they inhale, and then exhale as they trace down the finger. Continue until they've traced their entire hand. Now try with the other hand.

Ask students to create their own breathing exercises! Give students about two minutes to produce their own fun breathing styles. Afterward, partner students up to teach their partners their breathing style. Depending on time, have the students teach the whole class their partner's idea or join another group and teach their partner's idea.

After students have practiced each example of breathing, ask them to "rate" the technique from 1–5 stars, with 1 being "I didn't like it or find it helpful" and 5 being "I loved it, very calming." They can rate using their hands (holding up fingers to represent their answer).

ADDITIONAL ACTIVITIES

ELEMENTARY MIDDLE/HIGH

PROGRESSIVE MUSCLE RELAXATION

Ask students if they like Jello and what their favorite flavors are. Then, ask them to sit still and comfortably. They can look down or close their eyes. Inhale, and then, as you exhale, allow your feet to relax and go soft like jello. Now let your right leg go soft like jello. Inhale, and as you exhale, imagine your right knee is in a big bowl of jello. Now relax your left leg. Let it go soft and jiggly like jello. Imagine your left knee is in a jello mold.

Now relax your hips, letting them go soft like jello. Now relax your stomach. As you inhale, notice your stomach rising; as you exhale, let it fall and go soft.

Now relax your shoulders, let them slide away from your ears like Jello sliding around in a bowl. Imagine your soft relaxed shoulders in a jello mold.

Now relax your right arm, letting it go soft. Imagine your right hand in a jello mold, going soft and heavy. Now relax your left arm, letting it go soft. Imagine your left hand in a jello mold, going soft and heavy.

Now relax your face. Separate your back teeth and let your face go soft. Imagine your entire body just floating in a big mold of jello. Imagine your body is relaxed, soft, and supported.

ELEMENTARY

HOW MY BODY FEELS

Explain to students that our bodies send us signals when we start to feel frustrated. For example, some people notice their muscles tightening, their hearts racing, their palms sweating, or their faces turning red. Provide each student with paper and drawing materials and ask them to illustrate what happens in their own bodies as frustration builds. Encourage them to include any physical cues they experience—like a tight chest or sweaty palms—and to add a speech bubble showing common thoughts they might have when feeling upset (such as "This is too hard!" or "That's not fair!").

MIDDLE/HIGH

FIGHT, FLIGHT, FREEZE OR FAWN

Read each scenario and ask students to identify if it's an example of fight, flight, freeze, or fawn. Then, have them share a regulating or calming strategy they think that person could have used.

- You signed up for piano lessons as an elective, thinking it would be easy. However, you find the lessons much harder than expected and start venting loudly that you don't want to continue.
- You see a group of students teasing the new kid at lunch. You know it's wrong, but you feel unsure or uncomfortable and decide not to intervene or speak up.
- During class, some students start making fun of someone's haircut. Even though you realize it's unkind, you join in or laugh along.
- You discover that your younger sibling borrowed your phone without asking. Angry and annoyed, you end up yelling at them instead of calmly addressing the issue.
- You're asked to go to the principal's office for a disciplinary issue, but instead of facing the situation, you hide in the bathroom to avoid the meeting.
- You get called out for a classroom infraction, but you believe it's unfair. Instead of talking it through, you argue loudly with the teacher and refuse to listen.
- During the ACT, you encounter a difficult question. Feeling overwhelmed, you put your head down and stop working, giving up instead of attempting to move on.
- Your teacher calls on you to answer a question in front of everyone. You draw a blank and feel so embarrassed that you remain silent, unable to speak or ask for help.
- Your parents announce they're getting a divorce. Overcome by anger and sadness, you react by throwing your phone across the room.
- Your friend shows you a mean post they plan to share about another student. You know it's hurtful, but you decide not to say anything or try to stop them.
- You're struggling with a challenging math assignment. Your grandmother offers to help, but you're so frustrated that you snap at her instead of calmly explaining what you need.

CLOSING CONSIDERATIONS

When we experience strong emotions like fear, anger, or embarrassment, our amygdala—sometimes called our "alarm system"—can start "barking." If we don't pause to calm down, we might act in ways we later regret. The key is to notice how our body feels and use coping strategies, such as deep breathing, to settle our brains and bodies. Once we're calmer, our prefrontal cortex (PFC) can take over and help us make helpful choices.

How can what we practiced today help you in class or at home? How can it help you reach your goal?

Scaling Fist to Five

Ask students to reflect on today's session. Using their hands, ask them to put up the number that represents how they are feeling

- **0 (fist):** I feel totally overwhelmed and confused. I need lots of help.
- **3:** I understand it, but I need some support and practice.
- **5:** I feel confident. I could teach someone else all about this and how to do it.

"WOULD YOU RATHER?" GAME

Playing the "Would You Rather?" the game is a fun and engaging activity for students to develop their critical thinking skills. Students will reflect on their experience, evaluate their options based on their preferences, and reflect on the opinions of others, which provides different perspectives and strengthens the group's sense of connection to one another.

WOULD YOU RATHER?

Review cards before playing and remove any that may not be relevant or developmentally appropriate for your students. Copy and cut out the questions for small groups to discuss. You can also have students sit/stand or have each person stand in the center of the room and move toward one side or the other to show their vote for either option as the facilitator reads the questions aloud.

USE A FIDGET TOOL OR LISTEN TO MUSIC TO CALM DOWN?	TAKE A BREAK ALONE OR WALK WITH A FRIEND TO CALM DOWN?
DRAW ABOUT HOW YOU'RE FEELING OR SING ABOUT IT?	USE A RELAXATION APP TO HELP YOU CALM DOWN OR WATCH A FUNNY VIDEO TO LIFT YOUR MOOD?
DO YOGA OR STRETCH WHEN YOU FEEL FRUSTRATED OR RUN AND EXERCISE TO RELEASE YOUR ENERGY?	WRITE ABOUT HOW YOU ARE FEELING IN A JOURNAL OR TALK TO A FRIEND?

"It's okay to feel angry, but we can't let our anger control us."

UNKNOWN

CHAPTER 10

Self-Monitoring

MIND MAP

On the board, draw a mind map and ask students to consider the meaning of *Monitor*.

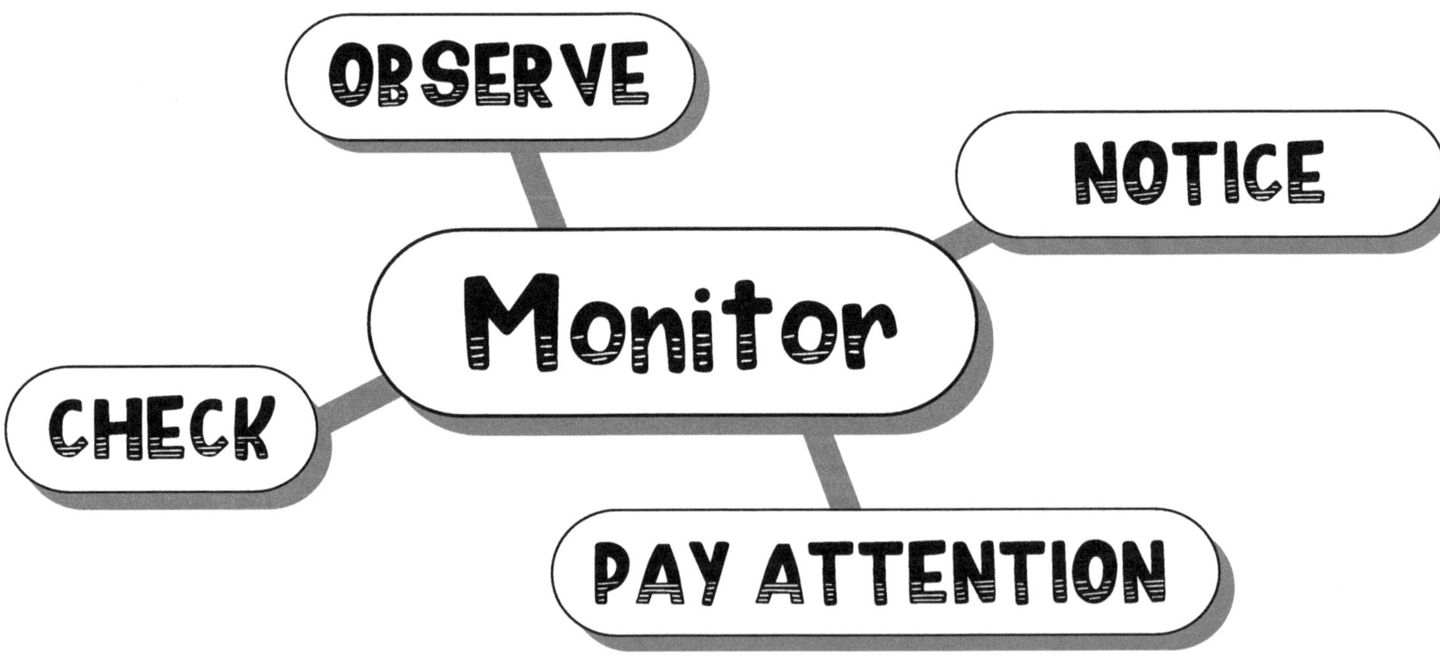

ASCA® STANDARDS

- **B-LS 4.** Self-motivation and self-direction for learning
- **B-LS 1.** Critical thinking skills to make informed decisions
- **B-SMS 1.** Responsibility for self and actions

DIRECTIONS

- Begin the group by asking members to share a **Peak** and **Pit** from their week.

Share a positive or high moment from the week. Something that made you smile or feel good.

Share a low from the week. How did you get through it?

Alternatively, students can use an emotion scale to rate their feelings on a scale of 1 (not feeling great) to 10 (feeling their best).

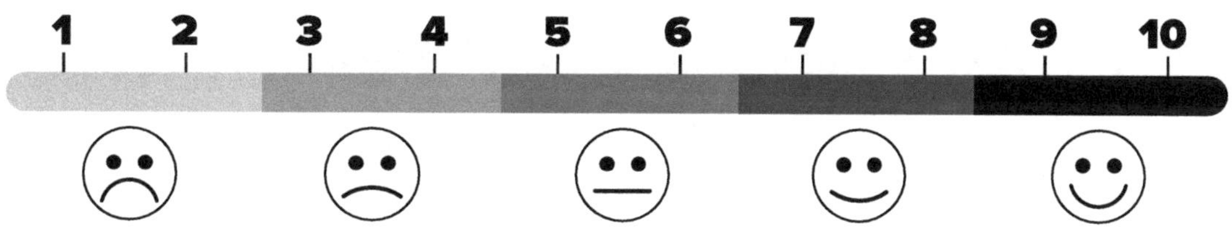

- Ask students to use the scale below to see how they're doing in reaching their goals. Our scale goes from 1 to 10: 1 means "I haven't started, or it's been really hard" and 10 means "I reached my goal!"

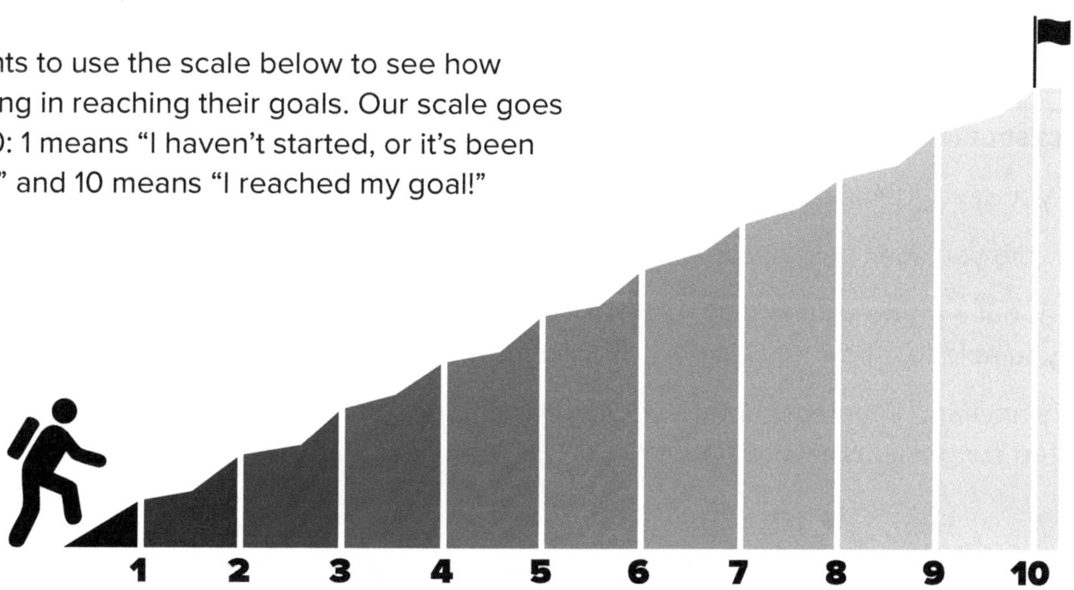

- Ask students to think about where they are on this scale and how they can move up? For example, if they're at a 4, what could they do to move up to a 5? Maybe they could try a new idea, ask a friend or adult for help, or change their plan. If they're at a 10, ask them to consider whether the goal was too easy. Could they try a bigger challenge next time?
- Review the Group Expectations.

- Read the Lesson Introduction and ask the Circle Time Questions before reading the Story and asking the Discussion Questions. Students can share individually or turn and talk to share their answers in pairs.
- Complete one of the Process Activities. If time allows, complete the Would You Rather cards (in a group or pairs) and Additional Activities.
- Be sure to complete the Closing Considerations with each lesson.

LESSON INTRODUCTION

Today, we're learning about self-monitoring, which means keeping track of how we're doing and how we're behaving. Each week, we've been checking in on our goals—that's one way we monitor our progress. We can also monitor our actions and behavior. For example, during group discussions, do you share the "airtime" so everyone gets a turn, or do you talk most of the time? Taking a moment to notice what's happening helps us become more self-aware and make better choices. We can do this by reflecting on what happened and thinking about how we want to act next time.

CIRCLE TIME QUESTIONS

Ask students to reflect upon and share their answers to the following questions with the group. Larger groups may need to be broken into smaller groups to give students ample time to share their answers and deepen the conversation.

- Reflect upon your journey toward meeting your goal by asking yourself:
    - What process/steps did you follow to work toward it?
    - What strategies did you use to overcome challenges?
    - Did you give yourself enough time and effort to achieve this goal?
    - How did you seek help or solve problems along the way?
- Think about a grade you recently received on an assignment. Were you satisfied with this grade? Were you able to "show what I know" through this assignment?
- Is there anything your teacher tells you over and over again when giving feedback? What patterns or repeated suggestions do you notice?

STORY TIME

Hand out the Coloring Sheets and crayons or markers to younger students while the facilitator reads the story, if desired.

Have students form a circle for the story activity and give one or two students a small object, such as a mini eraser or a marker. Explain that, as you read the story, they should pass the object to the left whenever they hear the word "**left**," and pass it to the right whenever they hear the word "**right**." Encourage them to listen carefully so they know which way to pass the object each time.

Left-Right Story: Ben's Busy Day

One morning, Ben walked into class and realized he had **left** his pencil at home. He looked **left** to see if anyone nearby had a spare, then glanced **right** to check if the teacher kept extra pencils. After a moment, the teacher gave directions for the writing assignment: "Dr. Seuss once said, "Think **left** and think **right** and think low and think high. Oh, the things you can think up if only you try!" write about what you think the quote means." But Ben got distracted by a drawing on the board. He turned **left** and **right** again to see what his classmates were doing, but they had already started working.

Ben looked **right** to see if anyone else was behind, but everyone was focused on their papers. *"What were the instructions?"* Ben wondered. He looked **left** for any notes on the board and saw the quote. Deciding he was short on time, he raced through the assignment anyway, scribbling down his answer as fast as he could.

When he finished, Ben looked **right** and realized no one else was done. *"I might have rushed,"* he thought. So, he turned **left** to read the directions carefully, then glanced **right** to see how his classmates were slowly double-checking their work. Taking a deep breath, Ben slowed down and went back through each problem step-by-step.

By the end of class, Ben felt proud that he had taken the time to understand the assignment. Now, whenever he's feeling lost or rushed, he remembers to look **left** and **right**, check the instructions, and pace himself so he doesn't miss any important details.

DISCUSSION QUESTIONS

- What caused Ben to lose focus and rush through his work?
- Do you relate to Ben by racing through assignments, or do you do the opposite by taking your time?
- What did Ben notice that helped him realize he needed to change his approach?
- How can double-checking your work help you do better?
- We were listening to the words "left" and "right" during the story. Did that make it easier or harder to focus on what was happening?

SKILL PRACTICE

Ask students to reflect on their experience in the group and how they felt about it overall. Then, hand out the **My Time in Group Self-Reflection Worksheet.**

Explain that they will privately rate themselves using a 1–5 star scale, where:

★ = Needs Improvement

★★★★★ = Exceptional

Each question is followed by five blank stars for students to fill in based on their self-assessment.

The reflection questions:

- I participated and stayed involved in group activities.
- I used a skill or strategy from this group to help me.
- I put in my best effort during group activities and discussions.

Encourage students to reflect on their experience by identifying one area where they *Glowed* (something they did well in the group) and one area where they could *Grow* (something they want to improve or would do differently in future groups or classes).

Have students write or draw their *Glow* and *Grow* in the designated boxes at the bottom of the worksheet. Let them know that their responses can be specific skills, participation, effort, or any other part of their group experience.

Once they finish, invite those who feel comfortable to share their reflections. Remind the group that sharing is completely voluntary—no one should feel pressured to speak if they'd rather keep their answers private.

ADDITIONAL ACTIVITIES

ELEMENTARY

LET'S LOOK AGAIN

Ask students to bring a recent assignment or piece of homework to reflect on or ask their teacher for a previous work sample. Have them spend time reviewing their work and noticing any mistakes or areas for improvement. Encourage them to think about whether those mistakes could have been prevented and what they might do differently next time. Then, invite students to share their reflections with the group, if they feel comfortable.

ELEMENTARY **MIDDLE/HIGH**

THE HUMAN KNOT

Explain to students that they'll be working together to solve a Human Knot—a fun teamwork and problem-solving activity! Form a circle with the group, or if doing as a class, break students into several groups. Everyone should reach across the circle and grab hands with two different classmates (not the people directly next to them). Make sure each student is holding hands with two *different* people.

Once everyone is connected, they'll have formed a "human knot" with their arms. The challenge is to untangle the knot—without letting go of hands! Students will need to twist, turn, duck, and step carefully to form one large circle again.

Group Size Tips:

- This activity works best with 6–10 students per group.
- If you have an odd number of students, one person may need to partner with someone already

holding one hand (so that one person is involved in three hands total), or you can rotate someone in as an observer or helper.

After the first round, ask students to self-reflect using a 1–5 scale, where 1 means they really struggled and 5 means they did exceptionally well. Encourage them to rate themselves in these areas:

- **Planning:** Did they think ahead or share ideas on how to untangle?
- **Communication:** Did they speak clearly and listen to their teammates?
- **Teamwork:** Did they cooperate and work together effectively?

Have students identify one or two ways they could improve based on their ratings. Then, let them try the activity again, applying their new strategies to see if they can improve their scores.

MIDDLE/HIGH

FLIP IT TO FIX IT: TURNING MISTAKES INTO MOTIVATORS

Inspired by the "Top Three Hits" activity by Noel Foy.[2]

Ask students to reflect on 2–4 common challenges they've faced—this could be mistakes they noticed in their behavior, habits that keep showing up, or repeated feedback from teachers, parents, or coaches.

Step 1: Identify the Pattern

Have them write down each challenge or piece of feedback they hear often. Examples might include:

- "I procrastinate."
- "I forget to turn things in."
- "I overreact when I'm frustrated."
- "I give up too quickly."

Step 2: Flip the Script

Now, for each challenge, they'll create a short reframing phrase—a sentence they can use as a reminder or mantra when that issue comes up again. These should be positive, action-focused, and short enough to write on a sticky note or say quietly to themselves.

Examples:

- "Do it now, not later."
- "Done is better than perfect."
- "Pause before I react."
- "I don't quit—I reset."

Step 3: Personalize It

Encourage students to choose one or two phrases that feel most meaningful and write them down somewhere they'll see them often—on a sticky note in a locker, a notebook cover, phone wallpaper, background image, etc.

CLOSING CONSIDERATIONS

Today, we talked about how pausing to check in with ourselves and self-monitor helps us stay on track and do our best work. By reflecting on what we've done afterward, we can spot both our strengths and the areas where we can improve. Making time for these skills now will set us up for success in the future.

How can what we practiced today help you in class or at home? How can it help you reach your goal?

Scaling Fist to Five

Ask students to reflect on today's session. Using their hands, ask them to put up the number that represents how they are feeling

- **0 (fist):** I feel totally overwhelmed and confused. I need lots of help.
- **3:** I understand it, but I need some support and practice.
- **5:** I feel confident. I could teach someone else all about this and how to do it.

"WOULD YOU RATHER?" GAME

Playing the "Would You Rather?" the game is a fun and engaging activity for students to develop their critical thinking skills. Students will reflect on their experience, evaluate their options based on their preferences, and reflect on the opinions of others, which provides different perspectives and strengthens the group's sense of connection to one another.

Would You Rather?

Review cards before playing and remove any that may not be relevant or developmentally appropriate for your students. Copy and cut out the questions for small groups to discuss. You can also have students sit/stand or have each person stand in the center of the room and move toward one side or the other to show their vote for either option as the facilitator reads the questions aloud.

TALK TO SOMEONE (LIKE A TEACHER OR PARENT) FOR FEEDBACK, OR REVIEW YOUR OWN WORK QUIETLY BEFORE ASKING FOR HELP?	BE THE FIRST ONE DONE BUT MAKE MISTAKES OR BE THE LAST ONE DONE BUT MAKE NO MISTAKES?
KEEP TRACK OF YOUR PROGRESS USING A CHECKLIST OR BY WRITING IN A DAILY JOURNAL?	LOOK BACK AT YOUR WORK TO SPOT MISTAKES ON YOUR OWN, OR ASK A FRIEND TO HELP YOU FIND THEM?
SET ONE BIG GOAL FOR THE WEEK AND SEE HOW YOU DO, OR SET SMALL DAILY GOALS AND CHECK THEM OFF EACH DAY?	KEEP TRACK OF YOUR FEELINGS WITH A MOOD CHART, OR TALK WITH A BUDDY EACH DAY TO CHECK IN ON HOW YOU'RE DOING?

"Slow and steady wins the race."

AESOP

MY TIME IN GROUP

Read the statements below and rate how you did by filling in the number of stars you would give yourself. Use the scale below as a guide.

★ = Needs Improvement

★★★★★ = Exceptional

- I participated and stayed involved in group activities.

  ☆☆☆☆☆

- I used a skill or strategy from this group to help me.

  ☆☆☆☆☆

- I put in my best effort during group activities and discussions.

  ☆☆☆☆☆

In the boxes below, write about one area where you really "Glowed" in Group, and one area where you feel you still have room to "Grow."

This is where I **GLOWED**	This is where I still have room to **GROW**

Final Group Session

LAST SESSION:

Directions & Overview

This final session is recommended, but optional. You may conclude the group during the final lesson topic if time does not permit this final session.

Directions: This final session is more relaxed and carefree, allowing students to spend time with one another and process their feelings about the group's conclusion. Facilitators may provide structured games or allow students to have unstructured time together.

Post-Group Expectations: Many students will have grown accustomed to meeting with you and will need reassurance about what support will be available after the group's conclusion. Be sure to review the protocol for meeting with you once the group has concluded.

Pre- and Post-Group Assessment: Ask students to complete the Post-Group Assessment. Review the directions aloud. Discreetly ensure that each student answered all questions when they return the forms.

Certificate of Completion: Present each student with their own Certificate of Completion. You can have as much or as little fanfare around this experience as you would like. Playing a song and asking students to stand and clap for their peers creates lasting memories for the participants.

Group Completion Letter: Give each student their Group Completion Letter to share with their caregiver, notifying them that the group has officially ended.

Group Conclusion: Ask each student to share what, if anything, this group has meant to them. Model this activity by sharing your experience as the group's facilitator.

Note to Facilitators: Consider ending with a "Warm Fuzzy" activity. If you like, begin by reading *The Original Warm Fuzzy Tale* by Claude Steiner[3] or referencing the Urban Dictionary definition. Emphasize that Warm Fuzzies are freely given—not earned or bought.

Provide each student with a set of note cards equal to the number of participants. Have them write their name at the top of each card, then pass one card to each group member. Everyone writes an encouraging message or positive affirmation on the card they receive. Students can also glue a fuzzy pom-pom next to their message.

For a non-writing option, give each student a handful of fuzzy pom-poms. As they share a compliment with a peer, they hand that peer a pom-pom. This simple exercise helps foster a supportive and caring atmosphere among the group.

ACTION PLAN

GRADE LEVEL

The curriculum is ideal for 2nd through 9th grade students.

GROUP TOPICS

- Executive Functioning Skills
- Setting Goals
- Planning/Prioritizing
- Organization
- Focus
- Recall and Memory
- Mindset
- Self-Regulation
- Managing Frustration
- Self-Monitoring

10-12 Sessions

Curriculum:
Use this Executive Function Workbook to facilitate your groups.

Materials:
Copies of the Assessments, Coloring Sheets, Activity Sheets, and "Would You Rather?" game, crayons or markers, pencils, and scratch paper.

Optional Materials: Windchime, highlighters, stopwatch (or use your phone), color dot stickers or Washi tape, cups, mini shredder, bubbles, music, note cards, and pom-poms.

NUMBER OF STUDENTS AFFECTED

Small group is ideal for 4–6 students who are struggling with executive functioning skills. These lessons can also be adapted to classroom lessons.

ASCA® STUDENT BEHAVIOR STANDARDS 18

M 1.	B-SMS 1.
M 3.	B-SMS 2.
M 4.	B-SMS 5.
M 5.	B-SMS 7.
B-LS 1.	B-SS 1.
B-LS 3.	B-SS 2.
B-LS 4.	B-SS 6.
B-LS 7.	B-SS 7.
B-LS 8.	B-SS 8.

ASCA® MINDSETS AND BEHAVIOR DATA

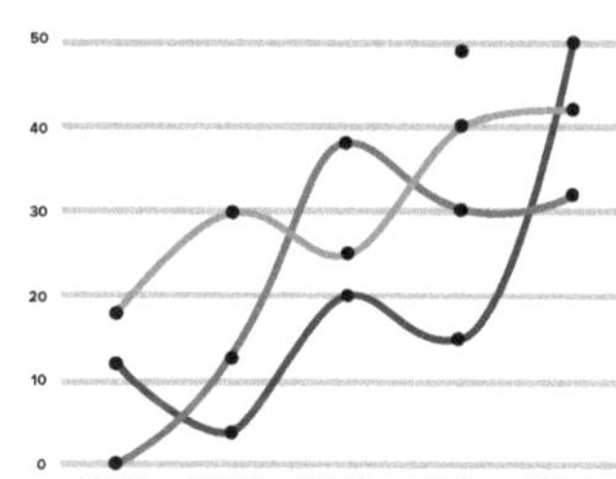

Use Executive Function pre- and post-assessment data to create a visual representation of their progress using their pre- and post-data.

OUTCOME DATA

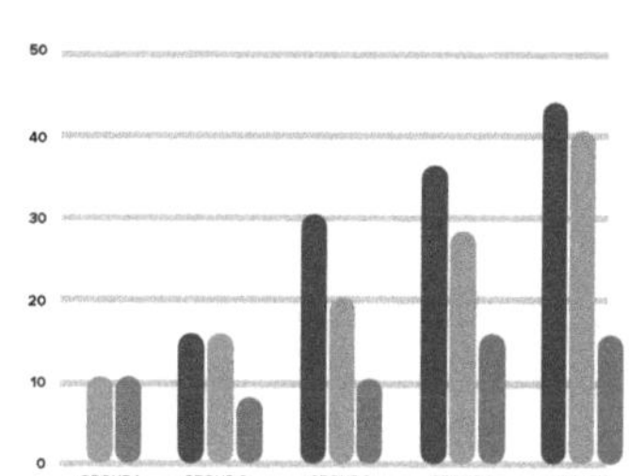

Use student achievement, attendance, or discipline data to measure students' progress to evaluate impact and effectiveness. Compare the pre- and post-data to answer the question "how did the learning affect student outcomes?"

EXECUTIVE FUNCTION GROUP PERMISSION FORM

Greetings, Caregivers of: ______________________________,

Your child is invited to participate in our **Executive Function Group**, a small-group program offered by the counseling department. We provide a range of services—classroom lessons, small groups, and individual sessions—to support student success. Students were invited to this group for various reasons, such as wanting help with time management, staying organized, completing tasks without procrastination, managing frustration, or developing a flexible, positive mindset. Referrals may come from students themselves, caregivers, or teachers. Please know, your student is not in any trouble, and being a part of this group in a positive way to help them continue to achieve their personal and academic goals.

In this group, we will explore how our brains help us plan, organize, prioritize, and set goals. We'll meet for about thirty minutes during the school day, once or twice a week, and I'll coordinate with your child's teacher to minimize classroom interruptions. When your child finishes all sessions, they will receive a Certificate of Completion.

At times, I may share information about your child's progress with relevant school staff—like their teachers, the social worker, or the principal—on a need-to-know basis, to ensure we provide the best possible support. All communication remains confidential within the school setting.

I'm excited to work with your child and help them strengthen these essential skills. If you have any questions or concerns, please feel free to contact me.

Warm regards,

✂- -

Please complete and return by: ______________________________

Student's Name: ______________________________

Teacher's Name: ______________________________

☐ YES, I agree to allow my child to attend the Executive Function Group.

☐ NO, I do NOT agree to allow my child to attend the Executive Function Group.

____

Signature of Caregiver

EXECUTIVE FUNCTION GROUP EXPECTATIONS

BE A MINDFUL LISTENER

Listen from your heart. When others are speaking, we all must do our best to focus on what others say with all our senses, wait your turn to speak, and keep our minds in the present without trying to decide what we will say next.

ACTIVELY PARTICIPATE

We are here to work together, so it is important that each one of us is doing our part to participate and engage. This will help us deepen our understanding of the topic, ourselves, and one another. When we fully dive into listening and participating, we will get more out of the group and grow stronger emotionally.

SHOW KINDNESS TO YOURSELF AND OTHERS

It is okay to disagree, but we won't yell or call each other names. We can support each other in keeping the space safe. This means we respond with curiosity, not criticism. We work hard to repair and restore our relationships if there is a conflict or disagreement.

BE WILLING TO LEARN AND GROW

In our group, we will create a safe space to share, make mistakes, and learn from each other.

WHAT IS SAID IN HERE, STAYS IN HERE

In our group, we will keep what we talk about confidential. Confidentiality means keeping what is said in the group private and not discussing it outside of the group. We know that some things are private, and not everyone needs to know about them. However, because we are a group, we can't promise that everyone will keep what you say private. If you share that you plan to hurt yourself or someone else or that someone is hurting you, I will keep you safe, but telling someone who needs to know can help keep you and others safe as well.

CREATE YOUR OWN

____

____

Group Attendance Form

Group:______________________________ Day/Time:________________________

	1	2	3	4	5	6	7	8	9	10	11	12
DATE												
	☐	☐	☐	☐	☐	☐	☐	☐	☐	☐	☐	☐
	☐	☐	☐	☐	☐	☐	☐	☐	☐	☐	☐	☐
	☐	☐	☐	☐	☐	☐	☐	☐	☐	☐	☐	☐
	☐	☐	☐	☐	☐	☐	☐	☐	☐	☐	☐	☐
	☐	☐	☐	☐	☐	☐	☐	☐	☐	☐	☐	☐
	☐	☐	☐	☐	☐	☐	☐	☐	☐	☐	☐	☐
	☐	☐	☐	☐	☐	☐	☐	☐	☐	☐	☐	☐

SESSION 1

SESSION 2

SESSION 3

SESSION 4

SESSION 5

SESSION 6

SESSION 7

SESSION 8

SESSION 9

SESSION 10

SESSION 11

SESSION 12

Group Attendance Form (Example)

Group: 5th Grade Lunch **Day/Time:** Thursday@12:30

	1	2	3	4	5	6	7	8	9	10	11	12
DATE	3/2	3/9	3/16	3/23								
Jane/Ms. W's Class	X	X	X	X	X	X	X	X	X	X	X	X
George/Mr. Day's Class	X	X		X	X	X	X	X	X	X	X	X
Sami/Ms. Smith's Class	X	X	X	X	X	X	X	X	X	X	X	X
John/Ms. Lee's Class	X		X	X	X	X	X	X	X	X	X	X
Malik/Ms. Lee's Class	X	X	X		X	X		X	X	X	X	X
Prishna/Ms. Smith's Class	X	X	X	X	X	X	X	X		X	X	X

SESSION 1	Intro/Assessment/Group Rules and Norms/Discussed expectations/Played game.
SESSION 2	What is Executive Function?
SESSION 3	Setting Goals
SESSION 4	Planning/Prioritizing
SESSION 5	Organization
SESSION 6	Focus
SESSION 7	Recall and Memory
SESSION 8	Mindset
SESSION 9	Self-Regulation
SESSION 10	Managing Frustration
SESSION 11	Self-Monitoring
SESSION 12	Check-ins/Assessment/Process group experience & Certificates awarded.

Pre- and Post-Assessment

My name is:______________________________

Date:______________________________

Executive Function Assessment

Circle 👍 if the statement is **true** for you.

Circle 👎 if the statement is **NOT true** for you.

There are no right or wrong answers!

Statement		
I understand what executive functioning is.	👍	👎
I set realistic short- and long-term goals and stick with them, even when it gets hard.	👍	👎
I usually create a plan before I start something new.	👍	👎
I use a system to keep my desk, backpack, and bedroom organized.	👍	👎
I can usually focus on what I'm doing and ignore distractions.	👍	👎
I am good at remembering directions and details.	👍	👎
I encourage myself to keep going when things get difficult, or when I make a mistake.	👍	👎
I am usually calm, alert, and ready to learn.	👍	👎
I use coping skills to manage strong emotions, like frustration.	👍	👎
I take time to check how things are going and make adjustments if needed.	👍	👎

Anything else you would like to share about the group? Write it below.

____

____

Results Report

Executive Function Assessment Data

GROUP GOAL:

STUDENT STATEMENTS:

Academic Results

Increase the total Benchmark scores/Reading Level following group intervention for group participation by ____%

____%

Attendance Results

Decrease the number of absences by ____% following group intervention for group participants

____%

Discipline Results

Decrease the number of conduct referrals by ____% following group intervention

____%

STUDENTS ATTENDED

NUMBER OF SESSIONS

OVERALL IMPROVEMENT

(See Formula Lower Right)

Pre-Assessment # True **Post-Assessment # True**

0

I understand what executive functioning is.

I set realistic short- and long-term goals and stick with them, even when it gets hard.

I usually create a plan before I start something new.

I use a system to keep my desk, backpack, and bedroom organized.

I can usually focus on what I'm doing and ignore distractions.

I am good at remembering directions and details.

I encourage myself to keep going when things get difficult, or when I make a mistake.

I am usually calm, alert, and ready to learn.

I use coping skills to manage strong emotions, like frustration.

I take time to check how things are going and make adjustments if needed.

OVERALL IMPROVEMENT FORMULA

$$\left(\frac{\text{Post-Assessment Total} - \text{Pre-Assessment Total}}{\text{Pre-Assessment Total}}\right) \times 100$$

Results Report (Example)

Executive Function Assessment Data

GROUP GOAL:

By the end of this twelve-session small group, participating students will demonstrate increased executive functioning skills—specifically in planning, organization, and self-regulation—by regularly using at least two new strategies in their daily routines.

STUDENT STATEMENTS:

"I am so proud of myself for meeting my goal."
"I'm so proud of how organized my backpack is."
"I learned all about being a responsible student."
"I really enjoyed our group."

Academic Results

Increase the total Benchmark scores/Reading Level following group intervention for group participation by 5 %

5 %

Attendance Results

Decrease the number of absences by 13 % following group intervention for group participants

13 %

Discipline Results

Decrease the number of conduct referrals by 10 % following group intervention

10 %

STUDENTS ATTENDED

6

NUMBER OF SESSIONS

12

OVERALL IMPROVEMENT

66.67%

(See Formula Lower Right)

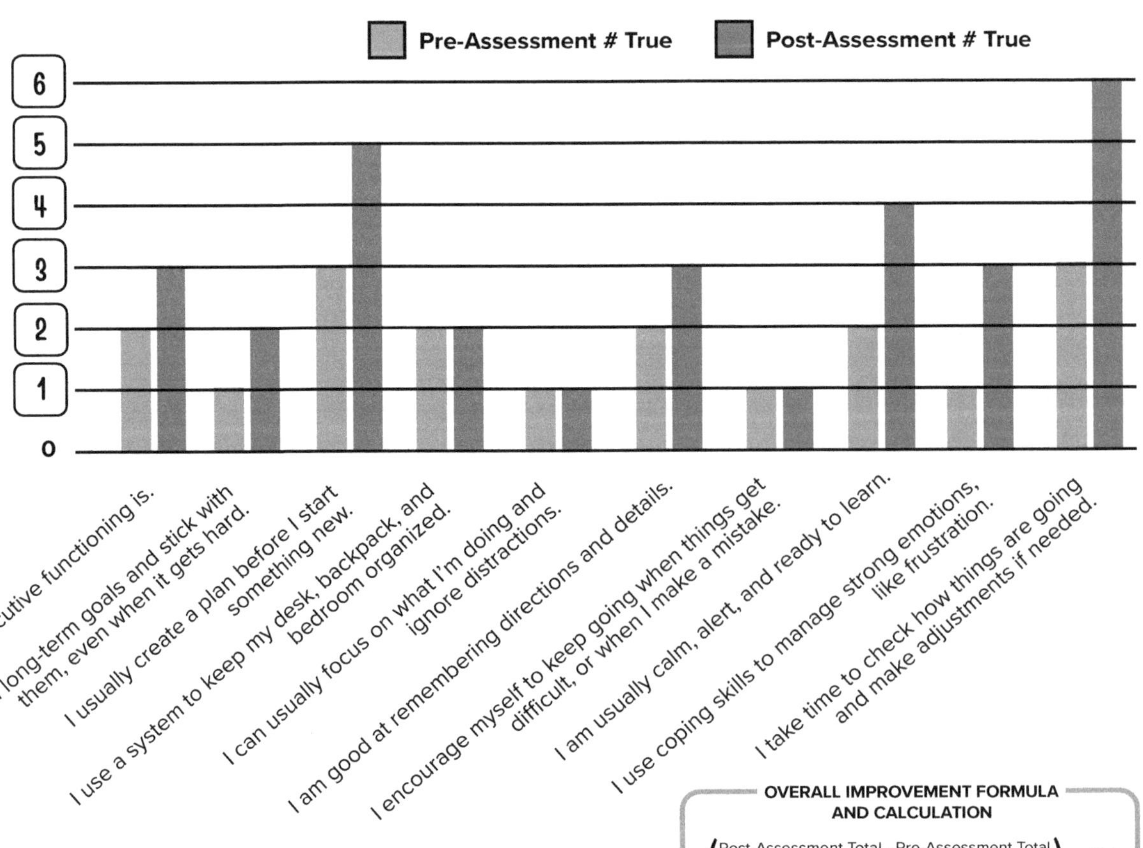

OVERALL IMPROVEMENT FORMULA AND CALCULATION

$$\left(\frac{\text{Post-Assessment Total - Pre-Assessment Total}}{\text{Pre-Assessment Total}}\right) \times 100$$

$$\left(\frac{30 - 18}{18}\right) \times 100 \qquad (.6667) \times 100 = 66.67\%$$

30-MINUTE GROUPS

CERTIFICATE

OF COMPLETION

This Certificate is Presented to:

____

For Participating in the **Executive Function Group**!

Facilitator: _______________________________

EXECUTIVE FUNCTION GROUP COMPLETION LETTER

Date:____________________________________

Dear ______________________________,

I'm writing to let you know that we just wrapped up our Executive Function Group, and your student has been awarded a Certificate of Completion!

Over the last ten sessions, we've explored important topics like:

- Executive Functioning Skills
- Setting Goals
- Planning/Prioritizing
- Organization
- Focus
- Recall and Memory
- Mindset
- Self-Regulation
- Managing Frustration
- Self-Monitoring

Although I'll still be available as their counselor, our weekly meetings have come to an end. If you have any questions or would like to discuss your student's progress, please feel free to reach out.

I'm very proud of all they've accomplished, and I appreciate your support in allowing them to take part in this group.

Warm regards,

____

School Counselor

ENDNOTES

1. James Clear, *Atomic Habits: An Easy Way to Build Good Habits & Break Bad Ones* (Penguin Random House, 2018), Chapter 5.
2. Noel Foy, *15-Minute Focus: Executive Function* (National Center for Youth Issues, 2025), p. 96
3. Steiner, Claude. *The Original Warm Fuzzy Tale*. Jalmar Press, 1977.

THE RESOURCES IN THIS BOOK ARE AVAILABLE FOR YOU AS A DIGITAL DOWNLOAD!

Please visit **ncyi.org/downloadable-resources** to access the downloadable resources.

Enter the code below to unlock the resources:

EXECUTIVE590

ABOUT THE AUTHOR

Laura Filtness, M.Ed., is a dedicated school counselor with over 15 years of experience exploring engaging activities and the power of books to support young minds in elementary classrooms. As a school counselor, she is passionate about fostering empathy and emotional growth in students. She also believes deeply that picture books are for everyone, no matter their age. Her therapy dog, Boss, inspired her debut picture book, *My Brain Is Like A Puppy*.

Laura has presented nationally on a variety of topics, including incorporating mindfulness into school programs, supporting students with ADHD, and using books and cooperative activities to transform lessons. She also holds multiple ASCA Specialist certifications.

Born in Coventry, England, Laura now lives in Knoxville, TN, with her two dogs, Brooklyn and Bindu. When she's not counseling or writing, she stays busy teaching yoga and Pilates, tackling endless home renovation projects, and watching anything and everything on TV.

NATIONAL CENTER for
YOUTH ISSUES

About NCYI

National Center for Youth Issues provides educational resources, training, and support programs to foster the healthy social, emotional, and physical development of children and youth. Since our founding in 1981, NCYI has established a reputation as one of the country's leading providers of teaching materials and training for counseling and student-support professionals. NCYI helps meet the immediate needs of students throughout the nation by ensuring those who mentor them are well prepared to respond across the developmental spectrum.

Connect With Us Online!

@nationalcenterforyouthissues

@ncyi

@nationalcenterforyouthissues